MASTER THE™ DSST®

Introduction
to
Geology Exam

About Peterson's

Peterson's® has been your trusted educational publisher for more than 50 years. It's a milestone we're quite proud of, as we continue to offer the most accurate, dependable, high-quality educational content in the field, providing you with everything you need to succeed. No matter where you are on your academic or professional path, you can rely on Peterson's for our books, online information, expert test-prep tools, the most up-to-date education exploration data, and the highest quality career success resources—everything you need to achieve your education goals. For our complete line of products, visit **www.petersons.com.**

For more information, contact Peterson's, 4380 S. Syracuse Street, Suite 200, Denver CO 80237; 800-338-3282 Ext. 54229; or visit us online at **www.petersons.com.**

ISBN-13: 978-0-7689-4467-9

Printed in the United States of America

10 9 8 7 6 5 4 3 2 1   23   22   21

Contents

Before You Begin

HOW THIS BOOK IS ORGANIZED

Peterson's *Master the*™ *DSST*® *Introduction to Geology Exam* provides a diagnostic test, subject-matter review, and a post-test.

- **Diagnostic Test**—Twenty multiple-choice questions, followed by an answer key with detailed answer explanations
- **Assessment Grid**—A chart designed to help you identify areas that you need to focus on based on your test results
- **Subject-Matter Review**—General overview of the exam subject, followed by a review of the relevant topics and terminology covered on the exam
- **Post-test**—Sixty multiple-choice questions, followed by an answer key and detailed answer explanations

The purpose of the diagnostic test is to help you figure out what you know—or don't know. The 20 multiple-choice questions are similar to the ones found on the DSST exam, and they should provide you with a good idea of what to expect. Once you take the diagnostic test, check your answers to see how you did. Included with each correct answer is a brief explanation regarding why a specific answer is correct, and in many cases, why other options are incorrect. Use the assessment grid to identify the questions you miss so that you can spend more time reviewing that information later. As with any exam, knowing your weak spots greatly improves your chances of success.

Following the diagnostic test is a subject-matter review. The review summarizes the various topics covered on the DSST exam. Key terms are defined; important concepts are explained; and when appropriate, examples are provided. As you read the review, some of the information may seem familiar while other information may seem foreign. Again, take note of the unfamiliar because that will most likely cause you problems on the actual exam.

After studying the subject-matter review, you should be ready for the post-test. The post-test contains sixty multiple-choice items, and it will serve as a dry run for the real DSST exam. There are complete answer explanations at the end of the test.

OTHER DSST® PRODUCTS BY PETERSON'S

Books, flashcards, practice tests, and videos available online at **www.petersons.com/testprep/dsst**

- A History of the Vietnam War
- Art of the Western World
- Astronomy
- Business Mathematics
- Business Ethics and Society
- Civil War and Reconstruction
- Computing and Information Technology
- Criminal Justice
- Environmental Science
- Ethics in America
- Ethics in Technology
- Foundations of Education
- Fundamentals of College Algebra
- Fundamentals of Counseling
- Fundamentals of Cybersecurity
- General Anthropology
- Health and Human Development
- History of the Soviet Union
- Human Resource Management
- Introduction to Business
- Introduction to Geography
- Introduction to Geology
- Introduction to Law Enforcement
- Introduction to World Religions
- Lifespan Developmental Psychology
- Math for Liberal Arts
- Management Information Systems
- Money and Banking
- Organizational Behavior
- Personal Finance
- Principles of Advanced English Composition
- Principles of Finance
- Principles of Public Speaking
- Principles of Statistics
- Principles of Supervision
- Substance Abuse
- Technical Writing

Like what you see? Get unlimited access to Peterson's full catalog of DSST practice tests, instructional videos, flashcards, and more for **75% off the first month!** Go to **www.petersons.com/testprep/dsst** and use coupon code **DSST2020** at checkout. Offer expires July 1, 2021.

Chapter 1

All About the DSST® Exam

WHAT IS DSST®?

Previously known as the DANTES Subject Standardized Tests, the DSST program provides the opportunity for individuals to earn college credit for what they have learned outside of the traditional classroom. Accepted or administered at more than 1,900 colleges and universities nationwide and approved by the American Council on Education (ACE), the DSST program enables individuals to use the knowledge they have acquired outside the classroom to accomplish their educational and professional goals.

WHY TAKE A DSST® EXAM?

DSST exams offer a way for you to save both time and money in your quest for a college education. Why enroll in a college course in a subject you already understand? For more than 30 years, the DSST program has offered the perfect solution for individuals who are knowledgeable in a specific subject and want to save both time and money. A passing score on a DSST exam provides physical evidence to universities of proficiency in a specific subject. More than 1,900 accredited and respected colleges and universities across the nation award undergraduate credit for passing scores on DSST exams. With the DSST program, individuals can shave months off the time it takes to earn a degree.

The DSST program offers numerous advantages for individuals in all stages of their educational development:

- Adult learners
- College students
- Military personnel

Adult learners desiring college degrees face unique circumstances— demanding work schedules, family responsibilities, and tight budgets. Yet adult learners also have years of valuable work experience that can frequently be applied toward a degree through the DSST program. For example, adult learners with on-the-job experience in business and management might be able to skip the Business 101 courses if they earn passing marks on DSST exams such as Introduction to Business and Principles of Supervision.

Adult learners can put their prior learning into action and move forward with more advanced course work. Adults who have never enrolled in a college course may feel a little uncertain about their abilities. If this describes your situation, then sign up for a DSST exam and see how you do. A passing score may be the boost you need to realize your dream of earning a degree. With family and work commitments, adult learners often feel they lack the time to attend college. The DSST program provides adult learners with the unique opportunity to work toward college degrees without the time constraints of semester-long course work. DSST exams take two hours or less to complete. In one weekend, you could earn credit for multiple college courses.

The DSST exams also benefit students who are already enrolled in a college or university. With college tuition costs on the rise, most students face financial challenges. The fee for each DSST exam starts at $100 (plus administration fees charged by some testing facilities)—significantly less than the $750 average cost of a 3-hour college class. Maximize tuition assistance by taking DSST exams for introductory or mandatory course work. Once you earn a passing score on a DSST exam, you are free to move on to higher-level course work in that subject matter, take desired electives, or focus on courses in a chosen major.

Not only do college students and adult learners profit from DSST exams, but military personnel reap the benefits as well. If you are a member of the armed services at home or abroad, you can initiate your post-military career by taking DSST exams in areas with which you have experience. Military personnel can gain credit anywhere in the world, thanks to the fact that almost all of the tests are available through the internet at designated testing locations. DSST testing facilities are located at more than 500 military installations, so service members on active duty can get a jump-start on a post-military career with the DSST program. As an additional incentive, DANTES (Defense Activity for Non-Traditional Education Support) provides funding for DSST test fees for eligible members of the military.

More than 30 subject-matter tests are available in the fields of Business, Humanities, Math, Physical Science, Social Sciences, and Technology.

Available DSST® Exams

Business	Social Sciences
Business Ethics and Society	A History of the Vietnam War
Business Mathematics	Art of the Western World
Computing and Information Technology	Criminal Justice
Human Resource Management	Foundations of Education
Introduction to Business	Fundamentals of Counseling
Management Information Systems	General Anthropology
Money and Banking	History of the Soviet Union
Organizational Behavior	Introduction to Geography
Personal Finance	Introduction to Law Enforcement
Principles of Finance	Lifespan Developmental Psychology
Principles of Supervision	Substance Abuse
	The Civil War and Reconstruction
Humanities	**Physical Sciences**
Ethics in America	Astronomy
Introduction to World Religions	Environmental Science
Principles of Advanced English Composition	Health and Human Development
	Introduction to Geology
Principles of Public Speaking	
Math	**Technology**
Fundamentals of College Algebra	Ethics in Technology
Math for Liberal Arts	Fundamentals of Cybersecurity
Principles of Statistics	Technical Writing

As you can see from the table, the DSST program covers a wide variety of subjects. However, it is important to ask two questions before registering for a DSST exam.

1. Which universities or colleges award credit for passing DSST exams?
2. Which DSST exams are the most relevant to my desired degree and my experience?

Knowing which universities offer DSST credit is important. In all likelihood, a college in your area awards credit for DSST exams, but find out before taking an exam by contacting the university directly. Then review the list of DSST exams to determine which ones are most relevant to the degree you are seeking and to your base of knowledge. Schedule an appointment with your college adviser to determine which exams best fit your degree program and which college courses the DSST exams can replace. Advisers should also be able to tell you the minimum score required on the DSST exam to receive university credit.

DSST® TEST CENTERS

You can find DSST testing locations in community colleges and universities across the country. Check the DSST website (**www.getcollegecredit. com**) for a location near you or contact your local college or university to find out if the school administers DSST exams. Keep in mind that some universities and colleges administer DSST exams only to enrolled students. DSST testing is available to men and women in the armed services at more than 500 military installations around the world.

HOW TO REGISTER FOR A DSST® EXAM

Once you have located a nearby DSST testing facility, you need to contact the testing center to find out the exam administration schedule. Many centers are set up to administer tests via the internet, while others use printed materials. Almost all DSST exams are available as online tests, but the method used depends on the testing center. The cost for each DSST exam starts at $100, and many testing locations charge a fee to cover their costs for administering the tests. Credit cards are the only accepted payment method for taking online DSST exams. Credit card, certified check, and money order are acceptable payment methods for paper-and-pencil tests.

Test takers are allotted two score reports—one mailed to them and another mailed to a designated college or university, if requested. Online tests generate unofficial scores at the end of the test session, while individuals taking paper tests must wait four to six weeks for score reports.

PREPARING FOR A DSST® EXAM

Even though you are knowledgeable in a certain subject matter, you should still prepare for the test to ensure you achieve the highest score possible. The first step in studying for a DSST exam is to find out what will be on the specific test you have chosen. Information regarding test content is located on the DSST fact sheets, which can be downloaded at no cost from **www.getcollegecredit.com**. Each fact sheet outlines the topics covered on a subject-matter test, as well as the approximate percentage assigned to each topic. For example, questions on the Introduction to Geology exam are distributed in the following way: Core Knowledge–30%, Surface Processes–30%, Tectonic Earth Processes–30%, and Applications–10%.

In addition to the breakdown of topics on a DSST exam, the fact sheet also lists recommended reference materials. If you do not own the recommended books, then check college bookstores. Avoid paying high prices for new textbooks by looking online for used textbooks. Don't panic if you are unable to locate a specific textbook listed on the fact sheet; the textbooks are merely recommendations. Instead, search for comparable books used in university courses on the specific subject. Current editions are ideal, and it is a good idea to use at least two references when studying for a DSST exam. Of course, the subject matter provided in this book will be a sufficient review for most test takers. However, if you need additional information, then it is a good idea to have some of the reference materials at your disposal when preparing for a DSST exam.

Fact sheets include other useful information in addition to a list of reference materials and topics. Each fact sheet includes subject-specific sample questions like those you will encounter on the DSST exam. The sample questions provide an idea of the types of questions you can expect on the exam. Test questions are multiple-choice with one correct answer and three incorrect choices.

The fact sheet also includes information about the number of credit hours ACE has recommended be awarded by colleges for a passing DSST exam score. However, you should keep in mind that not all universities and colleges adhere to the ACE recommendation for DSST credit hours. Some institutions require DSST exam scores higher than the minimum score recommended by ACE. Once you have acquired appropriate reference materials and you have the outline provided on the fact sheet, you are ready to start studying, which is where this book can help.

TEST DAY

After reviewing the material and taking practice tests, you are finally ready to take your DSST exam. Follow these tips for a successful test day experience.

1. **Arrive on time.** Not only is it courteous to arrive on time to the DSST testing facility, but it also allows plenty of time for you to take care of check-in procedures and settle into your surroundings.
2. **Bring identification.** DSST test facilities require that candidates bring a valid government-issued identification card with a current photo and signature. Acceptable forms of identification include a current driver's license, passport, military identification card, or state-issued identification card. Individuals who fail to bring proper identification to the DSST testing facility will not be allowed to take an exam.
3. **Bring the right supplies.** If your exam requires the use of a calculator, you may bring a calculator that meets the specifications. For paper-based exams, you may also bring No. 2 pencils with an eraser and black ballpoint pens. Regardless of the exam methodology, you are NOT allowed to bring reference or study materials, scratch paper, or electronics such as cell phones, personal handheld devices, cameras, alarm wrist watches, or tape recorders to the testing center.
4. **Take the test.** During the exam, take the time to read each question-and-answer option carefully. Eliminate the choices you know are incorrect to narrow the number of potential answers. If a question completely stumps you, take an educated guess and move on—remember that DSSTs are timed; you will have 2 hours to take the exam.

With the proper preparation, DSST exams will save you both time and money. So join the thousands of people who have already reaped the benefits of DSST exams and move closer than ever to your college degree.

INTRODUCTION TO GEOLOGY EXAM FACTS

The DSST' Introduction to Geology exam consists of 100 multiple-choice questions that assess students for knowledge equivalent to that acquired in an Introduction to Geology college course. The exam includes the following topics: Core Knowledge, Surface Processes, Tectonic Earth Processes, and Applications.

Area or Course Equivalent: Introduction to Geology
Level: Lower-level baccalaureate
Amount of Credit: 3 Semester Hours
Minimum Score: 400
Source: https://www.getcollegecredit.com/wp-content/assets/factsheets/IntroductionToGeology.pdf

I. **Core Knowledge – 30%**

   a. Earth Minerals: Minerals and Rocks

   b. Igneous Rocks: Intrusive, Extrusive

   c. Sedimentary Rocks: Characteristics, Interpretation

   d. Metamorphic Rocks

   e. Rock Cycle

   f. Plate Tectonics: Geomagnetics, Plate Boundaries, Plate Movements

II. **Surface Processes – 30%**

   a. Weathering and Soil

   b. Mass Wasting

   c. Streams and Floods

   d. Groundwater and Karst

   e. Glaciers and Glaciation

   f. Oceanic and Coastal Systems

   g. Deserts and Wind

   h. Hydrologic Cycle

III. **Tectonic Earth Processes – 30%**

   a. Geologic Time: Planetary Geology, Relative Time, Absolute Time, Field Relations

   b. Structural Geology: Folding, Faulting, Mountain Building

   c. Volcanoes and Volcanic Hazards

   d. Geophysics: Earthquakes and Seismology, Interior of the Earth, Gravity and Isostasy

IV. Applications – 10%

    a. Mineral and Energy Resources

    b. Environmental Geology

    c. Climate Change

Chapter 2

Introduction to Geology Diagnostic Test

DIAGNOSTIC TEST ANSWER SHEET

1. Ⓐ Ⓑ Ⓒ Ⓓ
2. Ⓐ Ⓑ Ⓒ Ⓓ
3. Ⓐ Ⓑ Ⓒ Ⓓ
4. Ⓐ Ⓑ Ⓒ Ⓓ
5. Ⓐ Ⓑ Ⓒ Ⓓ
6. Ⓐ Ⓑ Ⓒ Ⓓ
7. Ⓐ Ⓑ Ⓒ Ⓓ

8. Ⓐ Ⓑ Ⓒ Ⓓ
9. Ⓐ Ⓑ Ⓒ Ⓓ
10. Ⓐ Ⓑ Ⓒ Ⓓ
11. Ⓐ Ⓑ Ⓒ Ⓓ
12. Ⓐ Ⓑ Ⓒ Ⓓ
13. Ⓐ Ⓑ Ⓒ Ⓓ
14. Ⓐ Ⓑ Ⓒ Ⓓ

15. Ⓐ Ⓑ Ⓒ Ⓓ
16. Ⓐ Ⓑ Ⓒ Ⓓ
17. Ⓐ Ⓑ Ⓒ Ⓓ
18. Ⓐ Ⓑ Ⓒ Ⓓ
19. Ⓐ Ⓑ Ⓒ Ⓓ
20. Ⓐ Ⓑ Ⓒ Ⓓ

INTRODUCTION TO GEOLOGY DIAGNOSTIC TEST
24 minutes—20 questions

Directions: Carefully read each of the following 20 questions. Choose the best answer to each question and fill in the corresponding circle on the answer sheet. The Answer Key and Explanations can be found following this Diagnostic Test.

1. Rock is broken apart without a change in its composition by

   A. hydrolysis.
   B. carbonation.
   C. physical weathering.
   D. chemical weathering.

2. The sun and Earth formed directly from

   A. a protostar.
   B. a nebula of dust and gases.
   C. collisions between planetesimals.
   D. migration of extrasolar planets.

3. Which of the following has the highest carbon content and heating value?

   A. Anthracite
   B. Lignite
   C. Bituminous coal
   D. Peat

4. Which of the following characteristics are generally associated with mafic minerals?

   A. Dark in color, low density, crystals tend to be small
   B. Light in color, high density, crystals tend to be large
   C. Light in color, low density, crystals range in size from tiny to large
   D. Dark in color, high density, crystals range in size from tiny to large

5. A major component of soil is

A. bedrock.
B. sediment.
C. karst.
D. regolith.

6. If a newly formed rock contains 100 grams of a radioactive isotope, how much of the radioactive isotope would remain after two
half-lives have passed?

A. 0 grams
B. 25 grams
C. 50 grams
D. 75 grams

7. A rock can be best described as being a

A. consolidated assemblage of one or more types of minerals.
B. naturally occurring compound containing a single element.
C. mass that has the same chemical composition and physical
properties throughout.
D. set of atoms and molecules arranged in a regular, repeating
crystal lattice throughout.

8. Normal faults are associated with

A. tensional forces.
B. compressive forces.
C. shearing forces.
D. Coriolis forces.

9. A type of mass movement that occurs when a saturated mixture
of soil and regolith acts like a viscous fluid as it moves down a
slope is called

A. liquefaction.
B. a debris slide.
C. an earthflow.
D. creep.

10. Folded mountains are likely to form

    A. when plutons are emplaced in the crust.

    B. when a tectonic plate moves over a mantle plume.

    C. along a divergent plate boundary in a continent.

    D. along an oceanic–continental convergent boundary.

11. What is a major difference between gabbro and basalt?

    A. Basalt is much denser than gabbro.

    B. Basalt has smaller mineral crystals than gabbro.

    C. Gabbro is common at Earth's surface, but basalt is not.

    D. Gabbro and basalt have different chemical compositions.

12. Effusive volcanic eruptions are associated with

    A. violent explosions.

    B. extensive lava flows.

    C. highly viscous lava.

    D. large stratovolcanoes.

13. Greenhouse gases in the atmosphere increase temperatures by

    A. trapping outgoing infrared radiation in the atmosphere.

    B. blocking incoming infrared radiation from reaching Earth's surface.

    C. reflecting incoming infrared radiation back into space.

    D. delaying the escape of outgoing infrared radiation to space.

14. What type of landform is most likely to act as a drainage divide?

    A. Meandering stream

    B. Mountain range

    C. Floodplain

    D. Cut bank

15. The rock cycle is a set of processes that describe how

    A. tectonic plates interact with one another as they move over Earth's surface.

    B. chemical elements in Earth's interior and at the surface change into other elements.

    C. scientists classify minerals, identify their compositions, and group them into families.

    D. one type of rock can be transformed into another type of rock through natural processes.

16. Surface currents in the ocean are set in motion by

A. winds.
B. downwelling.
C. gyres.
D. waves.

17. What process does hot but mostly solid rock within the mantle undergo that allows for the movement of the overlying tectonic plates?

A. Convection
B. Subduction
C. Metamorphism
D. Lithification

18. Which scale is used to describe earthquake damage observed at different locations?

A. Richter
B. Moment-magnitude
C. Mercalli
D. Mohorovičić

19. Most of Earth's freshwater is contained in

A. groundwater.
B. streams and lakes.
C. clouds and precipitation.
D. glacial ice.

20. Which of the following is most likely to lead to the formation of a volcanic island arc?

A. A plate carrying oceanic crust subducts beneath a plate carrying continental crust.
B. A plate carrying continental crust subducts beneath another plate carrying continental crust.
C. A plate carrying continental crust subducts beneath a plate carrying oceanic crust.
D. A plate carrying oceanic crust subducts beneath another plate carrying oceanic crust.

ANSWER KEY AND EXPLANATIONS

1. C	5. B	9. C	13. D	17. A
2. B	6. B	10. D	14. B	18. C
3. A	7. A	11. B	15. D	19. D
4. D	8. A	12. B	16. A	20. D

1. **The correct answer is C.** The set of processes that breaks rock apart without a change in mineral composition is called physical weathering (also called mechanical weathering). Hydrolysis (choice A) and carbonation (choice B) are types of chemical weathering. In chemical weathering (choice D), chemical alterations take place within minerals, changing their composition.

2. **The correct answer is B.** The solar system originated from a nebula made of gases—mainly hydrogen and helium—and scattered dust grains. Choice A is incorrect because the sun, but no planets, originated as a protostar that formed at the center of the nebula. Collisions between planetesimals (choice C) led to the formation of the planets, but not the sun. The migration of extrasolar planets (choice D) was not involved in the formation of the solar system.

3. **The correct answer is A.** Anthracite, the highest grade of coal, contains the highest percentage of carbon and produces the most heat when burned. Lignite (choice B), the lowest grade of coal, has a relatively low carbon content and a low heating value. Bituminous coal (choice C) has a carbon content and heating value intermediate between lignite and anthracite. Peat (choice D), a precursor to coal, has the lowest carbon content and heating value.

4. **The correct answer is D.** Mafic minerals, which contain relatively low amounts of silica and high amounts of magnesium and iron, tend to be dark in color and have a higher density than felsic minerals. Their crystals can be of any size. Choice A is incorrect because mafic minerals tend to have a higher density than felsic minerals, and crystal size is not an indicator of whether a mineral is mafic or felsic. Choice B is incorrect because mafic minerals tend to be dark in color, and crystal size is not an indicator of whether a mineral is mafic or felsic. Choice C lists characteristics generally associated with felsic minerals.

5. **The correct answer is B.** Soil is the accumulation of fine materials—sediments weathered from rocks and organic matter—along with water and air. Bedrock (choice A) is unweathered rock. Karst (choice C) is a type of landscape that generally forms in carbonate rock. Regolith (choice D) is partially broken-up bedrock.

6. **The correct answer is B.** A half-life is the amount of time required for half of the atoms of a radioactive isotope to decay into a daughter isotope. In this example, after one half-life, 50 grams of the radioisotope would remain, and after two half-lives, 25 grams would remain. Choice A is incorrect because many half-lives would have to pass before all of the atoms of the radioactive isotope decayed. Half of the original amount (choice C) would be left after one half-life. Three-quarters of the original amount (choice D) would be present at a point within the first half-life.

7. **The correct answer is A.** A rock is made of an assemblage of various minerals or, less commonly, a single type of mineral. Choice B is incorrect because rocks are made of minerals, and although some minerals contain only one element, most are composed of a combination of elements. Choice C is incorrect because most rocks contain an assemblage of minerals that have varying compositions and physical properties. Choice D is incorrect because rocks are made of mineral crystals whose crystal lattices vary according to the minerals present. Even if a rock contains only a single mineral, it is likely that the individual crystals have different orientations.

8. **The correct answer is A.** Tensional forces, which act to pull the crust apart, result in the formation of normal faults. Compressive forces (choice B) result in the formation of reverse or thrust faults. Shearing forces (choice C) result in the formation of strike-slip faults. Coriolis forces (choice D) are unrelated to fault formation.

9. **The correct answer is C.** An earthflow forms when heavy rainfall or snowmelt saturates soil and regolith, and gravity causes the mass to flow downslope. Liquefaction (choice A) occurs when water-saturated sediments lose cohesion when shaken, causing the ground to act like a liquid. A debris slide (choice B) occurs when a mass of mainly soil and regolith slides downslope while remaining in a fairly coherent block. Creep (choice D), the slowest form of mass wasting, involves the gradual movement downslope of soil and regolith particles.

10. **The correct answer is D.** Compressive forces along an oceanic–continental convergent boundary cause folded mountains to form along the edge of the continent. Plutons (choice A) are emplaced as a result of igneous activity, which can accompany the formation of folded mountains but does not cause it. Choice B is incorrect because volcanic mountains form at the surface of a plate at a point directly over a mantle plume. Tensional forces along a divergent plate boundary (choice C) are likely to result in the formation of fault-block mountains.

11. **The correct answer is B.** Basalt is a fine-grained igneous rock that forms at Earth's surface; its extrusive counterpart is gabbro, which forms in Earth's interior. Basalt has smaller mineral crystals because it cools much more quickly from the molten state. Choices A and D are incorrect because basalt and gabbro have the same bulk composition. Choice C is incorrect because basalt is an extrusive igneous rock that forms at Earth's surface.

12. **The correct answer is B.** Effusive eruptions, in which large volumes of lava flow out onto and over the ground, are associated with shield volcanoes. Choices A and D are incorrect because explosive eruptions are associated with composite volcanoes, also called stratovolcanoes. Highly viscous lava (choice C) promotes the occurrence of explosive eruptions.

13. **The correct answer is D.** Greenhouse gases repeatedly absorb and reradiate energy at the longer wavelengths of the outgoing infrared radiation released from Earth's surface, delaying its escape to space and causing warming to occur. Choice A is incorrect because, although the passage of outgoing infrared radiation through the atmosphere is delayed by greenhouse gases, it is not trapped. Choices B and C are incorrect because reflecting incoming infrared radiation back into space, or blocking its arrival entirely, would cause cooling, not warming.

14. **The correct answer is B.** Drainage divides are ridges or other areas of relatively high elevations that define the boundaries of a drainage basin and separate adjacent drainage basins. Meandering streams (choice A), floodplains (choice C), and cut banks (choice D) are all low-lying features that may be present within a drainage basin.

15. **The correct answer is D.** The rock cycle is a set of natural processes through which igneous, sedimentary, and metamorphic rocks can undergo changes that transform them into other types of rocks. Choice A is incorrect because the rock cycle is only part of the processes involved as tectonic plates move. Choice B is incorrect because, except for processes involving radioactive decay, conditions on and inside Earth are not suitable for elements to change into other elements. Choice C is incorrect because the classification and identification of minerals is the field of mineralogy.

16. **The correct answer is A.** The frictional drag of winds across the top of the ocean sets surface currents in motion. Downwelling (choice B) involves vertical movement as dense surface water sinks. Gyres (choice C) are large, roughly circular patterns of flow of surface currents in the open ocean. Waves (choice D) transfer energy, not matter, through open water.

17. The correct answer is A. Plate movement is possible because of the circulation of convection currents within Earth's mantle. Subduction (choice B) is related to slab pull, thought to be the dominant process driving plate movement, but convection must be occurring for slab pull to take place. Choice C is incorrect because metamorphic processes are common at convergent plate boundaries but do not cause plate movement. Lithification (choice D) occurs as loose sediments are compressed or cemented to form sedimentary rock.

18. The correct answer is C. Values from I to XII on the Mercalli scale are assigned to describe observed earthquake damage at particular locations, from which the intensity of shaking caused by the earthquake is inferred. Both the Richter scale (choice A) and moment-magnitude scale (choice B) are logarithmic scales that produce a single numeric value to describe an earthquake's intensity. The Mohorovičić discontinuity (choice D) marks the boundary between the crust and uppermost mantle. It is unrelated to measures of earthquake damage.

19. The correct answer is D. Most of Earth's freshwater is contained as ice in glaciers. The second-largest amount is present as groundwater (choice A). Choices B and C are incorrect because only a small percentage is present at any one time in streams and lakes, or as clouds and precipitation, even though water constantly cycles among these reservoirs.

20. The correct answer is D. When an oceanic plate that is subducting beneath another oceanic plate becomes deep enough to start melting, the resultant magma can rise through the overlying plate and erupt to form a volcanic island arc. Subduction of an oceanic plate beneath a continental plate (choice A) leads to the formation of a continental volcanic arc near the edge of the continent. Choices B and C are incorrect because a plate carrying continental crust is not dense enough to subduct.

DIAGNOSTIC TEST ASSESSMENT GRID

Now that you've completed the diagnostic test and read through the answer explanations, you can use your results to focus your studying. Find the question numbers from the diagnostic test that you answered incorrectly and highlight or circle them below. Then, focus extra attention on the sections within Chapter 3 dealing with those topics.

Introduction to Geology		
Content Area	**Topic**	**Question #**
Core Knowledge	• Earth Materials: Minerals and Rocks • Igneous Rocks: Intrusive, Extrusive • Sedimentary Rocks: Characteristics, Interpretation • Metamorphic Rocks • Rock Cycle • Plate Tectonics: Geomagnetics, Plate Boundaries, Plate Movements	4, 7, 11, 15, 17, 20
Surface Processes	• Weathering and Soil • Mass Wasting • Streams and Floods • Groundwater and Karst • Glaciers and Glaciation • Oceanic and Coastal Systems • Deserts and Wind • Hydrologic Cycle	1, 5, 9,14, 16, 19
Tectonic Earth Processes	• Geologic Time: Planetary Geology, Relative Time, Absolute Time, Field Relations • Structural Geology: Folding, Faulting, Mountain Building • Volcanoes and Volcanic Hazards • Geophysics: Earthquakes and Seismology, Interior of the Earth, Gravity and Isostasy	2, 6, 8, 10, 12, 18
Applications	• Mineral and Energy Resources • Environmental Geology • Climate Change	3, 13

Chapter 3

Introduction to Geology Subject Review

OVERVIEW

- Core Knowledge
- Surface Processes
- Tectonic Earth Processes
- Applications
- Summing It Up

CORE KNOWLEDGE

This section of the subject review covers core geologic knowledge, including Earth materials, the rock cycle, and plate tectonics. Questions devoted to this content area account for 30 percent of the DSST exam.

Earth Materials

A **mineral** is an inorganic solid that forms naturally and has a definite chemical composition, a set of physical properties, and a regular, repeating crystalline structure. Some minerals contain only one element, but most are composed of a combination of elements. **Felsic minerals**, such as quartz, muscovite mica, and orthoclase feldspar, are richer in silica, generally lighter in color, and lower in density than mafic minerals. The term *felsic* derives from a combination of *feldspar* and *silica*. **Mafic minerals** have a lower silica content and are richer in magnesium and iron than felsic minerals. The term *mafic* derives from a combination of *magnesium* and *ferric* (a Latin term for iron). Mafic minerals generally have higher melting points and are higher in density than felsic minerals.

Minerals are classified into groups called **families** according to their composition. The largest is the **silicate family**, which contains minerals in which silicon is combined with additional elements. Examples include quartz, amphibole, feldspars, and clay minerals. The **carbonate family** contains minerals whose composition includes carbonate in combination with other elements. Examples include calcite and dolomite. In the **sulfate family**, sulfate is combined with other elements. In the **sulfide family**, sulfur combines with elements other than oxygen. Pyrite is a sulfide mineral. In the **halide family**, such elements as chlorine, fluorine, and iodine are combined with a metallic element. A major halide mineral is halite, which we use as table salt. The **oxide family** contains oxygen bound with a metallic element. Hematite is an oxide. **Native element minerals** are those containing only one element, such as gold or copper.

Minerals are the building blocks of rocks. A **rock** is a consolidated assemblage of minerals, or sometimes an assemblage of a single mineral. For example, granite is a rock composed mainly of quartz and feldspar, together with other, more minor, minerals. Limestone can be composed solely of calcite.

Rocks are classified according to how they form. The three groups of rocks are as follows:

1. Igneous
2. Sedimentary
3. Metamorphic

Igneous Rocks

Igneous rocks have cooled from a molten state—either from magma or lava. **Magma** is molten rock within Earth, and **lava** is molten rock that has erupted onto the surface.

Igneous rocks are generally classified according to the types of minerals they contain, which is determined by the composition of the molten rock from which they form and their **texture** (size of their mineral crystals), which is controlled by the cooling history. The three compositional categories of igneous rocks are as follows:

1. **Felsic igneous rocks:** rich in felsic minerals
2. **Intermediate igneous rocks:** a mix of felsic and mafic minerals
3. **Mafic igneous rocks:** rich in mafic minerals

Because mafic minerals have a higher melting/cooling point than felsic minerals, they crystallize sooner in the cooling process. The order in which minerals crystallize is described by the **Bowen reaction series**.

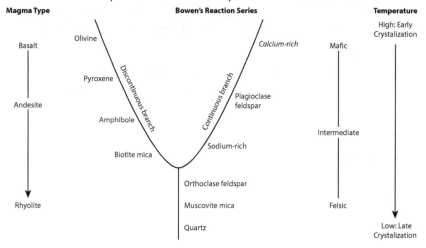

Figure 1: Bowen's Reaction Series

Due to the insulation provided by the surrounding rock, magma cools more slowly than lava. As such, rocks formed from cooled magma are more coarse-grained (have larger mineral crystals) than rocks formed from cooled lava, which have a fine-grained or even glassy texture.

Intrusive Igneous Rocks

Magma that is lower in density than the rock surrounding it will rise, pushing into and through the rock. Therefore, igneous rocks formed from cooled magma are called **intrusive**. They are coarse-grained, which means their mineral grains are visible without magnification. Granite is a common intrusive igneous rock that forms from silica-rich magma, so it has a felsic composition. Gabbro is another common intrusive igneous rock derived from a relatively silica-poor magma, which means it has a mafic composition.

Extrusive Igneous Rocks

When the magma that would produce coarse-grained rock as an igneous intrusion instead erupts at the surface as lava, it cools much more quickly. The result is a fine-grained **extrusive igneous rock**. The extrusive counterpart to granite is a quick-cooling, fine-grained rock called rhyolite. Cooling that is especially quick prevents the rock from forming well-crystallized minerals, resulting in a volcanic glass called obsidian. If this lava freezes while gases are rapidly escaping from it, myriad voids are preserved in the rock, producing pumice. Pumice can be light enough to float on water.

Molten rock that would produce gabbro if emplaced intrusively will instead produce a fine-grained extrusive rock called basalt. Basalt forms the ocean floor and also erupts on land. A lava with a basaltic composition that produces a glassy rock with numerous voids is called scoria.

Sedimentary Rocks

Characteristics

Sedimentary rocks are generally made of particles broken off of pre-existing rocks, called **sediment**, that have subsequently been naturally pressed together or cemented by newly precipitated minerals. These are called **clastic sedimentary rocks**. They may also form from organic materials such as shells, which can be compacted and compressed into a rock called limestone, or the carbon-rich remains of ancient plants, which can eventually be transformed into coal by heat and pressure.

Clastic sedimentary rocks contain pieces of earlier-formed rocks. These sediments undergo erosion and are transported to new locations. Agents of erosion include moving water, glaciers, and wind. When an erosional agent loses the capacity to transport sediment, the sediment is deposited.

Chemical sedimentary rocks form as minerals that had been dissolved in water precipitate, becoming solid again and building up into large deposits. This process is common in the ocean and mineral-rich lakes.

The process by which deposits of clastic or chemical sediments form sedimentary rock is called **lithification**.

Interpretation

Sedimentary rocks form at Earth's surface, and they record information about the conditions and environment that were present at the time the sediments were deposited. Because sediments are laid down in layers, called **beds** or **strata**, with the oldest ones at the bottom, changes in a location's environment over time can be reconstructed by observing the evidence contained in vertically stacked sedimentary beds—the **strati-graphic record**.

The size of grains of sediment in a deposit indicate the level of energy present in the environment when the grains settled out of water or wind. Fast-moving water is capable of transporting larger sizes of sediment than wind. Accumulations of pebble-sized or larger sediments show that at one time, the location was characterized by a high-energy environment, such as a fast-flowing mountain stream, from which only coarse-grained sediments could settle. Lithification of such a deposit produces a rock called a **conglomerate**.

Deposits of sand-sized grains show that water or wind transported the grains in an environment of moderate energy. Lithified deposits of sand become **sandstone**. Sometimes, ripples formed as sand migrated along a surface, such as a beach or stream channel, are preserved in sandstone as ripple marks.

Fine-grained sedimentary rocks such as **shale** indicate deposition in a low-energy environment. The particles of silt and clay minerals that form shale are quite small, so they can only settle in water or air that is still, or perhaps barely moving. Otherwise, they would continue to be transported until they reached a more suitable location for their deposition. Therefore, shale often forms from deposits laid down at the bottom of a deep lake or deep part of the ocean. Another sedimentary rock that indicates a low-energy environment is coal, which formed from ancient plant remains that accumulated in swamps. Fine-grained sedimentary rocks sometimes preserve mud cracks that formed when surficial sediments became desiccated and shrank in volume. Mud cracks can form as a pond dries up or when a tidal flat is exposed at low tide.

Additional environmental information can be gleaned by examining readily visible fossils of plants and animals, as well as microscopic materials such as pollen grains, incorporated into sedimentary strata. If pollen grains yield information about the types of plants growing in the region when the sediments were deposited, then a great deal of information about the climate at the time can be deduced—for example, how wet or dry it was and what the temperature range was. Plant and animal fossils also show whether a location was on land, in a freshwater environment (such as a lake or swamp), or covered by the ocean. By knowing something of the living requirements of organisms that leave fossil evidence, we can further describe the environment extant at the time the organisms lived.

Metamorphic Rocks

Metamorphic rocks have been transformed from igneous or sedimentary rock, or a different kind of metamorphic rock, generally by experiencing increased heat and/or pressure that causes their minerals to **recrystallize**. More intense levels of metamorphism can result in the formation of completely new minerals in place of the old ones, using the elements present in the original minerals as building blocks.

The type of rock from which a metamorphic rock forms is called the **parent rock**. Metamorphosis occurs when a parent rock is subjected to chemical or physical conditions that are markedly different than the ones in which it originally formed and then changes to come into equilibrium with its new environment.

Low-grade metamorphism causes small changes to a parent rock, such as shale transforming to slate. Bedding planes and fossils visible in the original shale may be retained in slate. At the other extreme, high-grade metamorphism causes changes so profound that it might not be possible to identify what the parent rock was. Although metamorphism, especially high-grade metamorphism, may occur at temperatures approaching the melting temperature of the rock, it never becomes hot enough for the rock to actually melt. If melting occurs, the end result is an igneous rock, not a metamorphic one.

Metamorphic agents include the following:
- Heat
- Pressure
- Chemically active fluids

These agents can act individually or in any combination.

Heat causes minerals to recrystallize, which results in the growth of larger crystals or the formation of completely new ones as chemical bonds break and re-form. The amount by which the temperature increases affects which minerals are transformed. For example, clay minerals start to recrystallize into minerals such as chlorite and muscovite mica at fairly low temperatures. More durable minerals, such as quartz and the feldspars, must be subjected to much higher temperatures before recrystallization begins.

Heat can be supplied by the emplacement of an igneous intrusion within the crust or by a surficial lava flow. The rocks bordering the magma or lava undergo **thermal metamorphism**, also called **contact metamorphism**. Heat also increases when subsidence and burial increase the depth in the crust at which a body of rock is located. Much of the deformation of rock that takes place during mountain-building episodes occurs at high temperatures and pressures within the crust. This large-scale metamorphism is called **regional metamorphism**.

Along with temperature, pressure increases with depth. **Confining pressure** is pressure that is applied equally in all directions. The confining pressure a body of rock is subjected to increases as the thickness of the overlying rock increases. High confining pressures force mineral grains closer together, eliminating any voids between them. The rock becomes more compact and therefore denser. High confining pressures also lead to the recrystallization of the original minerals into new minerals that take up less space.

Differential stress occurs when pressure is not the same in all directions. It is common, for example, for rocks to undergo differential stresses during mountain-building episodes. In the direction of greatest stress, the rocks are shortened. They lengthen in the perpendicular direction. Differential stresses lead to the formation of metamorphic textures characterized by the size, shape, and arrangement of mineral grains within a metamorphic rock.

Chemically active fluids are made of water that contains an abundance of ions and dissolved volatile substances (those that become gases under surface conditions). These fluids can cause parts of some minerals subjected to high stress to dissolve. The minerals then precipitate where the stress is lower. This process causes minerals to recrystallize and elongate in the direction perpendicular to the direction of maximum stress. As chemically active hot fluids circulate through the crust, they can exchange ions with the rocks they pass through. If extensive enough, this ion exchange will alter the overall composition of the rocks.

Metamorphic rocks can display either a foliated or nonfoliated texture. Features characteristic of a **foliated texture** include the following:
- **Parallel alignment** of platy (flat) minerals such as the micas
- **Compositional banding**—the separation of light- and dark-colored minerals into discrete bands
- **Cleavage**—a property that allows a rock to be readily split along flat planes.

A **nonfoliated texture** is characterized by randomly oriented mineral grains. Lack of foliation indicates that a metamorphic rock has undergone at most only minor deformation and may also have a limited chemical composition. For example, the contact metamorphism of a limestone predominantly composed of calcite results in the formation of marble, in which calcite has recrystallized and formed larger grains. Quartzite results from the contact metamorphism of quartz-rich sandstone.

Foliation reflects the level of metamorphism that has occurred. Consider a parent rock of shale. Low-grade metamorphism turns it into slate. The tendency of slate to undergo cleavage is useful in the manufacture of roofing and flooring tiles. As metamorphism continues, slate becomes **phyllite**, a shinier rock whose platy minerals have grown larger. Phyllite in turn transforms to **schist**, a medium- to coarse-grained rock in which mica minerals are abundant and that is easy to split. High-grade metamorphism changes schist to **gneiss**, a coarse-grained rock with compositional banding. Quartz and the feldspars are common minerals in gneiss, although they contain smaller amounts of other minerals.

Rock Cycle

Over geologic time, rocks undergo many changes—they form, break apart, re-form, melt, cool, and are metamorphosed. These processes are summarized in the **rock cycle**, which identifies how each type of rock forms and can change into another type of rock.

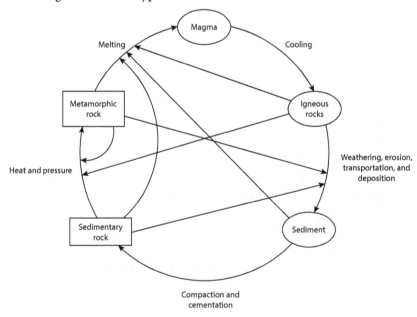

Figure 2: Rock Cycle

Rocks do not follow any set path as they move through the rock cycle. An intrusive igneous rock can undergo uplift to Earth's surface, where it can disintegrate into sediments over time. Alternatively, it might melt and cool again to form another igneous rock or be subjected to heat and pressure that turns it into metamorphic rock. A sedimentary rock can break apart into particles of sediments that are transported, deposited, and lithified into new sedimentary rock many times before moving to another stage of the rock cycle. Likewise, a metamorphic rock can be transformed into a different type of metamorphic rock without first becoming a sedimentary or igneous rock.

Plate Tectonics

Earth's outer layer, the **lithosphere**, is broken into huge slabs called **tectonic plates** that slowly move to new positions and form new configurations over geologic time. As the plates move, they interact along their boundaries in various ways, including causing rock to deform and fold, pushing up mountain ranges, and causing volcanic activity and earthquakes to occur.

The upper part of the lithosphere, the **crust**, is made of rock that is cool enough to behave in a brittle manner. The two types of crust are continental (which comprises the continents) and oceanic (which comprises the ocean floor). The bulk composition of **continental** crust is granitic. **Oceanic crust** is basaltic, so it is denser than continental crust. A tectonic plate can carry both continental and oceanic crust. At some plate boundaries, tectonic plates carrying oceanic crust sink into Earth's interior at plate boundaries called **subduction zones**, and at some others, new oceanic crust is created at plate boundaries called **seafloor spreading centers**. (Continental crust is not dense enough to be recycled in this way.) The planet's surface has been deformed, and oceanic crust has been destroyed and re-formed many times over billions of years by tectonic activity.

Geomagnetics

Earth's magnetic field affects the orientation of iron-rich mafic minerals, such as magnetite, as they form in cooling magma or lava. These minerals record the orientation of Earth's magnetic field at the time they solidified. Rocks that indicate what the orientation of the magnetic field was thousands or millions of years ago contain a record of **paleomagnetism**.

The paleomagnetic record shows that Earth's magnetic field has reversed direction many times over the planet's history. In other words, the magnetic north pole has become the magnetic south pole, at which time the magnetic south pole has become the magnetic north pole. At the next magnetic reversal, the magnetic poles resume the orientation we are familiar with today, which we call **normal polarity**. The opposite orientation is called **reverse polarity**. Magnetic reversals occur at irregular intervals.

At a seafloor spreading center, basaltic lava erupts and cools to form new oceanic crust. Magnetic minerals align with the current magnetic field as they form. Because oceanic crust forms symmetrically on either side of a spreading center, the youngest crust is always along the spreading center. As the plates on either side of the spreading center move apart, new lava erupts and cools, adding to the trailing edges of both plates. As a result of this process, oceanic crust becomes progressively older with distance from the spreading center at which it formed.

Some portions of oceanic crust formed during times of normal polarity, and some formed during times of reverse polarity. The result is the formation of **magnetic stripes** of varying widths in the seafloor that are symmetrical on either side of the spreading center (see Figure 3).

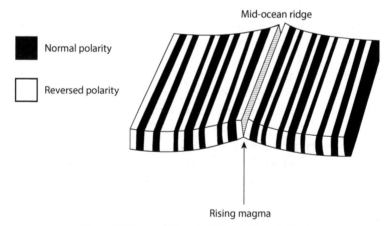

Figure 3: Patterns of Magnetic Stripes in Oceanic Crust

Seafloor crust that formed during times of normal polarity registers on a magnetometer as having a stronger magnetic field because its field is aligned with Earth's. Seafloor crust that formed during times of reversed polarity registers as having a weaker magnetic field. The pattern of symmetric magnetic stripes in the seafloor provides important evidence that supports the theory of plate tectonics.

Plate Boundaries

As tectonic plates move, they interact at their boundaries by pulling apart (diverging), pushing together (converging), or sliding horizontally (transforming) past one another.

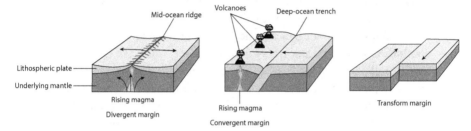

Figure 4: Types of Plate Boundaries

Divergent boundaries are those where plates are pulling apart as they move in opposite directions. Most divergent boundaries are in the ocean. Divergent plate boundaries are also called **constructive margins** because the rise of molten material to the surface results in the formation of new crust.

At an oceanic divergent boundary, erupting basalt forms new oceanic crust at a spreading center, which is marked by the presence of a linear chain of underwater mountains and volcanoes that form a mid-ocean ridge. At the center of the ridge is a **rift valley**. Newly formed oceanic crust is constantly being moved away from the rift valley by seafloor spreading. The ridge in the middle of the Atlantic Ocean is called, appropriately enough, the **Mid-Atlantic Ridge**. This ridge rises above the surface of the ocean to form Iceland, and it is one of the few places where seafloor spreading processes can be observed on dry land.

At a continental divergent boundary, known as a **continental rift**, the continent is slowly being pulled apart. Eventually, if rifting continues long enough, the continent will separate into two smaller continents, and a new ocean will form between them. The **East African Rift** system is an example of where modern-day continental rifting is occurring. The Red Sea is a location where the process is further along, leading to the formation of a narrow ocean.

Convergent boundaries are ones where plates are pushing together as they move toward each other. A convergent plate boundary can also be called a **destructive margin** because of the sinking and recycling of oceanic crust taking place along them. A convergent boundary can be a(n):

- Oceanic-oceanic convergent boundary
- Oceanic-continental convergent boundary
- Continental-continental convergent boundary

Along an **oceanic-oceanic convergent boundary**, two plates carrying oceanic crust push together. The older plate, which is colder and therefore denser, sinks at an angle beneath the younger one in a process called **subduction**. Subduction occurs in a subduction zone, which is a long, linear feature in the ocean floor, marked at the surface by a **deep-ocean trench**. One example is the **Marianas Trench** in the western Pacific Ocean. The deepest point of the seafloor, which is deeper than Mount Everest is high, resides in this trench. The sinking oceanic plate is progressively heated as it descends into the warmer region of the planet's interior below the lithosphere. Eventually, it reaches a depth where it begins to melt. This partial melting generates magma buoyant enough to rise through the plate that remains at the surface and erupt through volcanoes on the seafloor of the overriding plate. (Some of the magma also solidifies within the lithosphere, forming intrusive igneous rock.) If the volcanoes grow tall enough, their peaks emerge above the surface of the ocean and form a chain of islands known as a **volcanic island arc**. The **Aleutian Islands** of Alaska, which parallel the Aleutian Trench, are an example of a young volcanic island arc system. The volcanic activity at an oceanic-oceanic boundary is accompanied by earthquakes.

Along an **oceanic-continental convergent boundary**, a plate carrying oceanic crust collides with a plate topped with continental crust. The oceanic plate, being denser, subducts beneath the continental plate. Because the oceanic plate sinks at an angle, when it is hot enough for partial melting to occur, it is located underneath the continent. Some of the magma generated by partial melting can rise through the overlying continent and erupt through volcanoes, forming a **continental volcanic arc**. The **Andes Mountains** of South America contain many such volcanoes, along with mountains that thrust upward as the collision between the plates causes rock to bend and fold. As with an oceanic-oceanic boundary, earthquakes are common at an oceanic-continental convergent boundary.

Along a **continental–continental convergent boundary**, two plates topped with continental crust push together after the ocean between them has been destroyed by subduction. Neither continent subducts because of the relatively low density of continental crust. Even though there had been a subduction zone present, where the oceanic part of one plate was subducted as the continents approached each other, subduction ceases once the continents collide. However, the plates continue to push together, leading to the formation of a mountain belt, such as the Himalayas, a product of the collision between India and Asia. As a result of this ongoing collision, the Himalayas include the world's tallest mountain, Mount Everest. Because there is no subduction along a continental-continental convergent boundary, no magma is being generated, so no new volcanic activity occurs. Earthquakes, however, are common.

Transform boundaries are those where plates are neither pulling apart nor pushing together, but instead are moving horizontally past one another. Transform plate boundaries are also called **conservative margins** because no new material is added to either plate, and no old material is destroyed. The motion occurring at a transform boundary takes place along a feature known as a **transform fault**. Most transform boundaries are located in the ocean, but a few cut through continents. For example, the **San Andreas fault system** in southern California is a transform boundary that separates the Pacific Plate from the North American Plate. Because there is no subduction along a transform boundary, no magma is generated, so no volcanoes form. The movement of the plates along the transform fault marking their borders causes earthquakes to occur.

Plate Movements

Tectonic plates move at rates of centimeters per year. One way to measure the direction and speed of plate movement is to use GPS satellite data collected over many years. Over time, changes in the positions of locations that have been determined with high precision allow the calculation of plate movements.

Plate movement is possible because of convection within Earth's **mantle** below the lithosphere. **Convection** is a process by which heat is transferred by the movement of material. The very top of the mantle is cool and forms the lower part of the lithosphere. Deeper in the mantle, however, temperature and pressure conditions are such that rock can sluggishly deform and flow, even though it mainly remains in the solid state. This ability to flow sets up convection currents in the mantle, which carry hotter mantle materials higher as they rise and cooler materials deeper as they sink. Hot, rising material encounters progressively cooler temperatures as its depth decreases, causing it to cool and become denser. It eventually becomes dense enough to sink deeper into the mantle, completing the loop of the convection current. Where neighboring convection currents rise and diverge under the lithosphere, divergent plate boundaries form; where neighboring currents converge and sink, convergent plate boundaries form.

Processes driving plate movements include slab pull, mantle drag, and ridge push. **Slab pull** is thought to be the dominant process. Because a cold, sinking oceanic plate is denser than the hot mantle below it, gravity pulls the plate downward. **Mantle drag** can enhance or impede plate movement, depending on whether the portion of the mantle underlying a plate is flowing more quickly or slowly than the plate is moving. **Ridge push** is also related to the action of gravity. Because a mid-ocean ridge forms an elevated region in the seafloor from which the plates on either side move away, the plates "slide" down the ridge toward the lower elevations of the adjacent seafloor.

In addition to the magnetic patterns discovered in oceanic crust and GPS data, evidence of plate movements includes the distribution of volcanoes. Most volcanoes form at divergent or convergent plate margins, but some form far from any plate boundary, in either the ocean or on a continent, as a result of **intraplate volcanism**. An example is the **Hawaiian Islands**, which are located in the interior of the Pacific Plate. Intraplate volcanism occurs where a column of hot mantle material, called a **mantle plume**, rises and acts like a blowtorch on the base of the overlying tectonic plate. The resultant partial melting that occurs, along with melting of some of the plume material that takes place when it encounters the lower pressures present at shallower depths, generates basaltic magma that can rise through the plate and erupt through volcanoes as lava.

An intraplate volcano can continue to erupt as long as it is situated over the mantle plume. If an intraplate volcano is located on the seafloor and grows tall enough via sequential eruptions, its top becomes an oceanic island. The Hawaiian Islands formed in this manner. Only the island that is currently over the mantle plume hosts active volcanoes. As the Pacific Plate moves, it slowly but steadily carries an island away from the mantle plume. The island loses its source of magma, and its volcanoes become extinct. This process causes a well-defined relationship in the ages of the islands: Age increases with distance from the point on the seafloor above the mantle plume. The youngest island is currently above the plume, and the other islands become increasingly older the farther they are away from that point. Determining the islands' ages and measuring the distance between them allows the direction and speed of plate movement to be determined.

SURFACE PROCESSES

This section of the subject review covers surface processes, such as weathering, wasting, streams, floods, groundwater, glaciers, coastal systems, deserts, wind, and the hydrologic cycle. Questions on this topic account for 30 percent of the DSST exam.

Weathering and Soil

Rocks that are at or near Earth's surface undergo **weathering**, which breaks rock into smaller pieces or dissolves susceptible minerals in water. Weathering occurs in place—it does not include **erosion**, which is the transport of materials. In some places, unweathered bedrock may be exposed in an outcrop at the surface. However, in most places, the upper part of the bedrock has been partially broken up, producing **regolith**. As the regolith continues to undergo weathering, it forms the parent material from which soil develops, along with any other sediments that are deposited in the area.

Weathering

Weathering processes are classified as either physical or chemical. **Physical weathering** (also called **mechanical weathering**) occurs when rocks are broken apart without a change in the composition of their minerals. The freeze-thaw cycle provides an example of this type of weathering, called **frost wedging**. As liquid water freezes into ice, its volume increases. When this occurs in cracks in rocks, the cracks are slightly enlarged. Over time, repeated freeze-thaw cycles result in rocks breaking apart. A similar process called **salt crystal growth** occurs in coastal regions and arid regions. As salt crystals grow in cracks in rocks, the crystals slowly force the cracks wider, eventually breaking the rocks into smaller pieces. Because physical weathering increases rocks' surface area by breaking them apart, it increases the availability of surfaces on which chemical weathering can act.

Chemical weathering causes minerals in rocks to decompose because of the chemical alteration taking place when minerals are exposed to water and air. As elements are added or removed, the internal structure of a mineral as well as its composition changes. The presence of water is needed to facilitate the chemical reactions involved in chemical weathering. Although physical weathering attacks cracks and voids in rocks, chemical weathering is capable of dissolving and changing minerals throughout rocks.

One example of chemical weathering is **oxidation**, which involves the formation of an oxide mineral, such as when iron combines with oxygen to form iron oxide, also known as **rust**. Iron oxide is soft and crumbles easily, enhancing the breakdown of rocks. Another example is **hydrolysis**, in which silicate minerals such as the feldspars combine with water, leading to the formation of clay minerals. Yet another example is **carbonation**, which occurs as minerals react with **carbonic acid**, a weak acid that forms naturally as carbon dioxide in air combines with water from rain or melted snow and ice. Carbonate minerals, such as calcite, are particularly vulnerable to the effects of acids, which dissolve them. Over time, carbonation can lead to the creation of vast caverns in limestone.

Climate has a strong effect on weathering rates. Annual precipitation rates, annual temperature patterns, and the frequency of freeze–thaw cycles are all important factors. Physical weathering is the dominant process in regions with dry, cool climates. Arid conditions, such as in desert climates, greatly slow rates of weathering. Chemical weathering is dominant in wet, warm climates because the chemical reactions involved occur more quickly as temperature and water supply increase. Under hot and wet conditions, such as in some equatorial climates, weathering rates are rapid, and weathering processes extend far below Earth's surface.

Soil

Soil is the accumulation of fine materials—both mineral and organic matter, along with water and air—in which plants grow. The characteristics of a soil determine its fertility or ability to support plant growth. Soils develop from regolith, which in turn develops from a parent rock—the type of bedrock present in an area. When a soil is fairly young, its mineral composition shows the identity of the parent rock.

The thickness of soil from the surface to the lowest point plant roots reach, or to the point where regolith or bedrock begins, is called a **soil profile**.

Each distinct layer in a soil profile is called a **soil horizon**. The boundaries between horizons are recognizable by a change in soil properties, such as color, texture, presence or absence of particular minerals, and moisture content. A well-developed soil profile in a humid temperate region commonly has five horizons: O, A, E, B, and C.

The **O horizon** is at the top and is composed mainly of organic material from plants and animals that has been transformed by its partial decomposition into a material called **humus**. Biological activity is high in humus. The layers below the O horizon are mainly composed of mineral matter. The next layer down is the **A horizon**, which contains some humus and in which biological activity is also high. **Topsoil** is the material contained in the O and A horizons.

Below the A horizon is the **E horizon**, which is lighter in color and contains little organic matter. It is mostly made of coarse sand, silt, and weathering-resistant minerals. As water percolates through the E horizon, it carries finer particles downward in the process of **eluviation**. The water dissolves soluble materials and carries them downward as well. This removal of material to lower horizons is called **leaching**. Higher rates of precipitation lead to higher rates of eluviation and leaching.

Below the E horizon is the **B horizon** where materials such as clays removed by eluviation from the E horizon accumulate. The B horizon is also referred to as the **subsoil**. Together, the O, A, E, and B horizons comprise the **solum**, or true soil. Soil-forming processes are active in the solum, and this region contains plant roots and animal life. Below the subsoil of the B horizon is the **C horizon**, which contains regolith. Unweathered bedrock underlies the C horizon.

Soils are often studied in units called **pedons**. A pedon consists of a hexagonal column extending into the ground. Its sides form cross-sections in which soil horizons can be seen. Pedons in an area can be grouped into **polypedons**, which are the soil units shown on maps of soil distributions.

Mass Wasting

A **mass wasting** event occurs when gravity acts on surface material causing it to move down a slope. This occurs when the force of gravity overcomes the cohesiveness of surficial materials and the internal friction that acts to hold them in place. Steeper slopes are more susceptible to mass movement of surficial materials. The slope's steepness strongly influences how far the material moves and where it stops moving. Freely moving granular material comes to rest at its **angle of repose**—i.e., the steepest angle at which the material can be piled without slumping. The size and shape of the grains determines the angle of repose.

The four basic classifications of mass movement are falls, slides, flows, and creep.

A **fall** occurs when individual, detached pieces of any size travel at a high rate of speed down a very steep slope, and may undergo free fall through the air, before hitting the surface below. When a quantity of rock falls through the air, the event is called, appropriately enough, a **rockfall**. A rockfall from a cliff results in an accumulation of irregularly shaped, broken rocks at the bottom of the cliff in a pile called a **talus cone**. A rockfall or earthquake can trigger a **rock avalanche**, in which large numbers of rocks tumble downslope, repeatedly colliding with other rocks as well as the slope. As it continues to move downslope, a rock avalanche initiated by a rockfall can be considered to transition to an event more like a rapid flow of material.

A **slide** occurs when surface material remains in a fairly coherent block as it moves downslope over a well-defined surface, such as a bedding plane that is approximately parallel to the slope. A **rockslide** or **debris slide** occurs when a mass of rock, or a mass of mainly soil and regolith, slides downslope. In a **slump**, the material moves along a curved surface.

A **flow** occurs when surface material acts like a viscous fluid as it moves down a slope. A flow is commonly saturated with water. A mixture of water, soil, and regolith comprises a **debris flow**. When the material is predominantly fine-grained, it is called a **mudflow**. An **earthflow** can form when heavy rainfall or snowmelt saturates soil and regolith and moves downslope. An earthquake can cause a type of earthflow called **liquefaction** where water-saturated sediments lose cohesion when shaken, causing the ground to flow. Buildings can tilt or sink when the ground beneath them liquefies. A type of flow that originates on a volcano is called a **lahar**. The heat from a volcanic eruption can rapidly melt snow and ice that might be present at or near the top of a volcano. As this water mixes with sediments and volcanic debris, it forms a hot mudflow that can race downslope.

Creep, the slowest form of mass wasting event, involves the gradual movement downslope of soil and regolith particles. Any process that disturbs surface materials can facilitate creep, including the impact of raindrops and the actions of living organisms such as burrowing animals and roots. Freeze-thaw cycles can be important in promoting creep, depending on an area's climate. As water freezes beneath surface particles, its expansion slightly lifts the particles. When thawing occurs, the particles fall back to the surface at a slightly lower elevation. Therefore, each cycle results in particles undergoing a tiny downslope movement.

Streams and Floods

No matter its size or volume, a flowing body of water, including a river, can be called a **stream**. **Stream systems**, also called **fluvial systems**, occupy drainage basins. A **drainage basin** is an area of land where precipitation collects and drains into a particular body of water, such as a river or lake. Ridges or other areas of relatively high elevations, called **drainage divides**, define the boundaries of a drainage basin and separate adjacent drainage basins. The catchment area of a drainage basin is called a **watershed**.

As water moves through a stream system, it picks up or dissolves some of the materials it flows over, causing erosion. Deposition occurs when these materials come to rest or precipitate. Two measures of a stream's ability to move materials are competence and capacity. **Competence** refers to a stream's ability to move particles of a specific size. Competence increases as a stream's velocity increases. As velocity decreases, larger particles are deposited first, causing sediments to become sorted by size. **Capacity** refers to the total possible sediment load a stream is able to transport. It increases as a stream's volume increases.

A stream can move eroded materials in four ways: solution, suspension, traction, and saltation. **Solution** refers to the total load of dissolved sediments in a stream. The **suspended load** is all of the particles moving with the flow of the water above the stream bed. These particles are finer than ones moving along the bed, which make up the **bedload**. The coarser materials moving as bedload are dragged along the bed by **traction**, or they move by **saltation**—a process in which particles are briefly lifted above the bed and then fall out of suspension, causing them to move in a series of "hops."

In areas where the land slopes gently, a stream tends to form looping curves called **meanders**. Water flows more swiftly along the outer part of a meander, so it experiences erosion that can carve a steep bank called a **cut bank** into the landscape. Water moves slowly along the inner part of a meander, so it experiences deposition that can build up into a **point**

bar. Over time, the positions of the cut banks and point bars change as the meandering stream moves back and forth across the landscape. If the particulate load in a stream is greater than the stream's capacity, deposits of sediments build up in the stream channel. The stream becomes a set of interwoven, sediment-laden channels called a **braided stream**.

A stream will continue to erode sediments and cut down through a landscape until it reaches a **base level**—an elevation below which a stream cannot cause erosion. A base level can be local, such as when a mountain stream enters a lake. The upstream part of the stream cannot cause erosion to occur below the elevation of the lake surface. Globally, sea level is the ultimate base level.

The mouth of a stream is located where the stream reaches a base level, which is often a larger body of water. As the water leaves the stream channel, its flow is no longer restricted. The water spreads out and slows down, abruptly decreasing its capacity. The coarsest sediments are deposited first, and the finest sediments are carried farther. The depositional feature that forms at the stream's mouth is called a **delta**.

A **flood** occurs when a stream overflows its banks. The banks of a stream are natural (or, in some cases, artificially constructed) **levees** produced by flood events. As soon as a stream overtops its banks, the water spreads out and loses velocity. Coarse sediments (generally, sand-sized particles) are deposited adjacent to the channel, while fine sediments (generally, silt- and clay-sized particles) continue to be transported farther from the channel. As these sediments are deposited, they fill in the lowest areas first, leading to the formation of a relatively smooth, low-lying **floodplain** on either side of the channel. Successive flood events build the levees higher and add layers of fine sediment to the floodplain.

A meandering stream will move back and forth over its own floodplain deposits, changing its course over time. Sometimes, a meander is cut off from the rest of the stream, forming an **oxbow lake**. Eventually, an oxbow lake fills with sediment, becoming a **meander scar** on the floodplain.

An unusually large amount of water upstream can lead to or exacerbate flooding downstream. The severity of a downstream flood can be predicted by measuring upstream **discharge**—the volume of water moving down a stream per unit of time (often, per second). Discharge is determined by multiplying the water's velocity and the cross-sectional area of the channel (its depth multiplied by its width). To measure water depth, a pole called a **staff gauge** may be placed in a channel, frequently by attaching it to a bridge support. In addition, or alternatively, a device called a **stilling well** may be placed next to the stream and connected to it. Water from the stream is able to enter the stilling well, where the height of the surface of the stream surface is measured. Velocity measurements can be taken with current meters.

Groundwater and Karst

Groundwater is water that is present in saturated zones beneath Earth's surface, where it occupies voids and cracks in soil, sediment layers, and rock. The **water table** marks the upper surface of the saturated zone. Sediment layers and bodies of rock through which groundwater can flow (either because it is naturally permeable or is highly fractured) are called **aquifers**. Groundwater moves much more slowly than surface water. Groundwater is replenished when surface water percolates through the ground and reaches the water table.

Areas where the surficial bedrock is primarily composed of carbonate rock, such as limestone, may develop a **karst** landscape—one characterized by bumpy topography, poor surface drainage, and well-developed underground solution channels, all related to the chemical weathering of the limestone by carbonation. Large numbers of sinkholes and extensive underground caverns may be present. Streams may sink below the surface and then flow underground, forming what are called **disappearing streams**.

As chemical weathering dissolves limestone under the ground, the overlying surface may collapse, forming a **sinkhole**. Sinkholes are often roughly circular in shape at Earth's surface. When the surface is heavily pitted by sinkholes, the resulting landscape is referred to as **cockpit karst**. **Karst valleys** are larger features that may form as a result of surface dissolution or the collapse of the roof of an underground cavern.

When the water table is lower than part or all of a cavern, the cavern is filled with air, and calcium carbonate dissolved in groundwater can precipitate. Elaborate structures may build up: **stalactites** may hang from the ceiling, and **stalagmites** may jut from the floor. Sheets of limestone called **flowstone** may be deposited.

Glaciers and Glaciation

Formation and Structure of Glaciers

A **glacier** is a perennial mass of ice that is large enough to flow downslope due to the force of gravity. Glaciers are part of Earth's **cryosphere**—the portion of Earth's water and ground that remains perennially frozen. Continuous glaciers that cover huge land areas, as in Greenland and Antarctica, are called **continental glaciers**. Continental glaciers may be one of three types: ice sheets, ice caps, or ice fields.

An **ice sheet** is the largest type of continental glacier. **Ice caps** are smaller and roughly circular in shape. Both ice sheets and ice caps smother the underlying topography. **Ice fields** are smaller than ice caps and may have mountain peaks emerging above them. Relatively small glaciers that occupy mountain valleys are called **mountain glaciers** or **alpine glaciers**. When such glaciers are confined within a valley, they are called **valley glaciers**. When they emerge from the valley and spread out, they are called **piedmont glaciers**.

Glaciers begin to form as snow accumulates and survives year-round. The weight of subsequent snowfalls compresses the underlying snow, closing air pockets and increasing its density. Increasing pressure causes the snow to recrystallize into larger ice crystals with a granular texture, known as **firn**. The continued compaction of firn eventually produces glacial ice.

A glacier grows as it accumulates new snow and ice. It shrinks or ablates when it loses snow and ice, usually by melting. An **equilibrium line** separates the **zone of accumulation** from the **zone of ablation**. The equilibrium line migrates to higher or lower elevations as climate cools or warms. In addition to melting, a glacier can lose mass through sublimation or through **calving**—the breaking off of blocks of ice. **Icebergs** are created when a glacier calves into the ocean.

Glaciation and Erosion

A glacier acts like a huge bulldozer, picking up and moving material from one location and dumping it in another. A glacier can incorporate rocks the size of small pebbles or massive boulders by **plucking**, which occurs when meltwater at the base of the glacier refreezes around rocks, causing them to be "plucked" from the ground as the glacier moves onward. Once incorporated into the ice, material at the bottom of the glacier "sandpapers" the exposed rock it moves over in a process called **abrasion**. Abrasion by fine particles can smooth the surface of the underlying rock, causing it to display **glacial polish** when the ice retreats. Abrasion by larger particles can create grooves called **glacial striations** oriented parallel to the direction of flow.

The landscape beneath a glacier is profoundly changed in characteristic ways. Continental glaciers tend to grind down the entire landscape. Mountain glaciers produce distinctive landforms. A stream-cut valley is V-shaped, but the action of a glacier flowing down it transforms it into a **U-shape**. The glacier in the main valley is larger and causes more erosion. Smaller glaciers in tributary valleys carve out their valleys more shallowly. When the ice retreats, the higher tributary valleys become **hanging valleys** from which waterfalls may cascade into the main valley. Ridges separating glaciated valleys may be honed by erosion into sharp **arêtes**. When a mountain peak is gouged from all sides by glaciers, it is shaped into a pyramid called a **horn**.

A landform that forms from the erosion of bedrock and looks like an asymmetrical, streamlined hill is called a **roche moutonnée**. Its upstream side slopes gently and displays glacial polish, while the steep downstream side has been roughened by glacial plucking.

Glaciation and Deposition

A glacier can move material ranging from clay-sized particles to massive boulders. This jumble of glacially transported, unsorted sediment is called **glacial till** when it is deposited directly from the glacier. Till that is deposited along the sides of the glacier forms **lateral moraines**. When two separate glaciers meet and flow in a parallel manner, the lateral moraines along their boundary become a **medial moraine**. Till that is deposited at the front of the glacier that has reached an equilibrium position (where glacial advance and retreat are balanced) forms an **end moraine**. An end moraine that forms at the farthest extent reached by the glacier is called a **terminal moraine**. Till that is not piled into a lateral or end moraine but, instead, forms a widespread deposit as it drops from ice melting in place is called a **ground moraine**.

When a glacier retreats or melts in place, it leaves behind ground covered with unorganized deposits of glacial sediment that form a **till plain**. Till plains are typically characterized by low, rolling relief and deranged drainage patterns. Huge boulders left by a glacier are called **glacial erratics**.

A general term encompassing all forms of glacial deposits is **glacial drift**. It includes deposits of till as well as other deposits, called **outwash**, that have been further transported and sorted according to size by meltwater streams. A large area covered with outwash in front of a glacier is an **outwash plain**. Braided streams are common in outwash plains, as are water-filled depressions called **kettle lakes**.

A roche moutonnée is an erosional landform, but another type of stream-lined hill, known as a **drumlin**, is created by the deposition and molding of glacial sediments. As a continental glacier moves over already-deposited till, it can shape it into an elongated hill whose blunt end faces upstream and tapered end extends downstream. Groups of drumlins are called **drumlin swarms**.

Oceanic and Coastal Systems

The Oceanic System

Seawater contains large amounts of dissolved salts, the concentration of which is expressed as the water's **salinity**. The salinity of water in the open ocean is generally about 35 parts per thousand, which means that a kilogram of water contains 35 grams of dissolved salts. However, salinity values can vary dramatically near land.

The uppermost layer of the ocean is heated by the sun and mixed by the action of the winds blowing over the water. This **mixed layer** makes up only a tiny portion of the ocean's total volume. Below the mixed layer, the ocean is stratified by density. Located under the mixed layer is the **thermocline transition zone**, a region in which temperatures rapidly decrease as depth increases. In the deep ocean below the thermocline, temperature and salinity values are similar throughout. Even in tropical regions, temperatures in the deep ocean hover near 0°C. Due to its salinity, seawater freezes at about –2°C. Water never freezes in the deep sea.

Currents and Waves

The frictional drag of winds across the top of the ocean sets surface currents in motion. Deep currents are driven by density differences caused by variations in water temperature and salinity. The paths of currents are modified by the configuration of the seafloor and the locations of landmasses. Currents are deflected to the right in the Northern Hemisphere by the **Coriolis force** (a result of Earth's rotation) and to the left in the Southern Hemisphere. In both hemispheres, surface currents in the open ocean form large, roughly circular patterns of flow, called **gyres**.

Overall oceanic circulation is sometimes described as being a **global conveyor belt** of surface and deep currents that loop around the planet. **Downwelling** occurs as cold, dense surface water sinks in locations like the North Atlantic Ocean and around Antarctica. **Upwelling** occurs as water becomes less dense and rises, such as in the Indian Ocean and North Pacific, or when it is forced upward by a topographic barrier. After it returns to the surface, water is eventually carried by currents to a down-welling zone, where it sinks again. A compete circuit of the global conveyor belt takes about 1,000 years.

When winds transfer some of their energy to the ocean by frictional drag across its surface, they generate **waves**, which travel in groups called **wave trains**. The ocean is crisscrossed by wave trains that move in all directions. Storm winds generate large waves that may travel thousands of kilometers across the ocean before they break against a shore. It is important to note that waves transfer energy, not matter, through open water. Water molecules travel in circular patterns called orbits as the energy of a wave passes through. It is only when the water becomes shallow enough for the bottom of a wave to drag along the seafloor does the wave become a breaking wave, or **breaker**. As a breaker collapses, it carries energy, water, and sediment toward shore.

Tides

The changing orientation of the components of the Earth–Moon–Sun system causes ocean **tides** that are generally daily or twice-daily oscillations in sea level. A rising tide is called a **flood tide**, which reaches its maximum at **high tide**; a retreating tide is called an **ebb tide**, which reaches a minimum at **low tide**. The gravitational pull experienced by Earth from both the sun and moon generates high and low tides. The moon's influence is greater, even though it is much smaller than the sun, because the moon is much closer.

Both the moon and sun pull ocean water into **tidal bulges** on the near and far sides of the planet. These tidal bulges are aligned with and reinforce one another when the earth, moon, and sun are positioned in a straight line, which occurs during a new moon or full moon. At these times, the combined gravitational effects of the moon and sun produce what are known as **spring tides**, when the difference between high and low tides is greatest. When the earth, moon, and sun form a right angle, which happens during the first- and third-quarter phases of the moon, their gravitational influences are offset and interfere with one another, producing **neap tides** that have the least difference between high and low tides. From an astronomical standpoint, rather than tides rising and falling, the earth rotates in and out of the tidal bulges created by the moon and sun.

The difference in height between consecutive high and low tides defines a location's **tidal range**, which can be quite different at various locations and can vary throughout the year. The tidal range is affected not only by the generation of tides but also by the size and depth of a particular ocean region, the topography of the local seafloor, and the configuration of the shoreline.

Coastal Systems

The contact line between the ocean and land is called the **shoreline**. The land adjacent to the shoreline is known as the **coast**. The coastal environment, or **littoral zone**, contains both land and ocean areas. On land, it extends to the high-water line reached by the ocean during the most powerful storms. In the ocean, it extends to the depth where storm waves are no longer capable of moving seafloor sediments.

The action of waves breaking against the shoreline tends to cause an irregularly shaped coast to become straighter. Approaching waves slow when they reach shallower areas, such as around a headland, while continuing at their original speed in deeper water. This speed differential causes waves to bend, or refract, around headlands or large bodies of rock emerging above the ocean surface. This **wave refraction** concentrates wave energy and erosive power on headlands and other protruding landforms. As waves enter the progressively shallower bays and coves separating the headlands, they gradually lose energy, allowing sediments to be deposited. Therefore, the headlands erode landward over time, and the bays and coves fill with sediment.

Upwelling is a process that can occur when surface water is moved seaward from a coast, such as by offshore winds. Deeper, cooler water rises to replace the surface water that has been removed. This water is generally rich in nutrients that support the marine food web, leading to high biological productivity in coastal waters.

Beaches

A **beach** is the portion of land along a coast where sediment is being transported by ocean processes. Generally, the beach zone extends from a few meters above the high tide mark to a few meters below the low tide mark. Some beaches are stable year-round; others undergo seasonal cycles of summertime sediment accumulation during fair weather and wintertime erosion by storm waves. The sediments removed from the beach by winter storms are moved slightly offshore and deposited in the lower-energy, deeper environment. During low-energy summer periods, this sediment is gradually transported back onto the beach.

Quartz sand dominates most beaches for two reasons: (1) Quartz is the most abundant mineral on Earth's surface, and (2) it resists being broken down by weathering processes. Therefore, after most other minerals have been weathered into tiny particles of silt or clay, or dissolved, sand-sized grains of quartz remain. In areas with abundant volcanism, beaches may consist of dark-colored sediments broken from young volcanic rocks.

In the surf zone, a **longshore current** flows parallel to the coastline. It develops as a result of breaking waves that approach the land at an angle. Even though it is generally a weak current, the longshore current transports large quantities of sand and other sediments along the shore as **longshore drift**. Particles involved in longshore drift move in a zig-zag fashion along the beach as they are pushed landward by advancing waves and pulled seaward by retreating waves.

Coastal Erosion and Deposition

Coastlines can be characterized as being erosional or depositional, depending on which process dominates. An **erosional coastline** is likely to be present when a tectonic plate boundary is nearby. The tectonic activity can result in uplift of the land, leading to rugged topography, including sea cliffs. **Sea cliffs** form when wave action cuts notches into the land. The notches lead to the collapse of the rock above them, forming cliffs and causing them to retreat over time as notching continues. Additional erosional landforms are common along coastlines with sea cliffs, including sea caves and resistant rock that forms **sea arches**—openings eroded into detached or semi-detached rock. The eventual collapse of a sea arch leaves isolated pillars of rock in the water, called **sea stacks**.

A depositional coastline tends to be present when the land and adjacent seafloor slope gently and the sediment supply is abundant. Accumulations of sediment can build up several types of depositional landforms, including spits, tombolos, and barrier islands. A **spit** forms when sand is deposited in a long ridge that extends from a coastline. A body of sand connecting the shoreline with a nearby island or sea stack is called a **tombolo**. A **barrier island** is a long, narrow island located close to and oriented parallel to a shoreline. Barrier islands can be composed of deposits of sand and other sediments and can be large enough for towns to be built on them.

Corals, Salt Marshes, and Mangrove Swamps

Corals are simple marine animals called **polyps**. Polyps have a hard external skeleton formed from the calcium carbonate they secrete. Some types of corals are **colonial**, which means they live in large groups. In aggregate, colonial corals can produce huge structures, such as barrier reefs, made of calcium carbonate or limestone. Many types of colonial corals have photosynthetic algae called **zooxanthellae** that live within them. These corals must live in clear, sunlit waters so the algae can survive and photosynthesize. Polyps and zooxanthellae have a mutualistic relationship. Polyps provide a protected environment and compounds needed for photosynthesis, and the zooxanthellae provide polyps with photosynthetically produced food.

Because of their need for sunlight, colonial corals live near the surface of the ocean. Many generations of corals build upward on the limestone skeletons of older corals below them. The foundation of the reef may be the sides of a volcano, or the top of a submerged volcano. These reefs can form a fringing reef, barrier reef, or atoll. A **fringing reef** grows parallel to the coastline but is separated from the shore by a narrow, shallow lagoon. A **barrier reef** is similar to a fringing reef but is separated by a wider, deeper lagoon. An **atoll** is a ring of coral surrounding a central lagoon. An atoll is likely to form when an island surrounded by fringing reefs becomes submerged, such as by geological forces, or as sea level rises. Such islands are commonly the tops of oceanic volcanoes. If the submergence of the island occurs slowly enough for the growth of corals to keep up with it, the upward growth of the fringing reefs produces an atoll.

Salt marshes are coastal wetlands in which salt-tolerant plants grow. They are usually located north of 30° N or south of 30° S latitude in sheltered areas where fine-grained sediments can accumulate, such as estuaries or behind sand spits. As salt-marsh plants grow, they allow additional sediments to be trapped, leading to an increase in the area occupied by the salt marsh.

Mangrove swamps are groups of mangrove trees and other salt-tolerant plants that grow in tropical and subtropical environments located in a band centered on the equator. The northern boundary of this band is roughly 30° N latitude, and the southern boundary is roughly 30° S latitude. The distribution of mangrove swamps is constrained by the occurrence of freezing temperatures, which mangrove seedlings cannot survive. Sediments that accumulate along a coastline in a sheltered area provide an opportunity for the establishment of a mangrove swamp. The roots of mangrove trees form mazes in the water that provide habitat for numerous other marine organisms.

Corals, salt marshes, and mangrove swamps all provide buffers between the open ocean and the coastline that absorb energy from high-energy storm waves and help protect the coastline from erosion.

Deserts and Wind

Deserts

Deserts are regions of persistent aridity. Although deserts are commonly thought of as being covered by sand, their surfaces are frequently characterized by desert pavements, especially in subtropical areas. **Desert pavement** resembles a cobblestone street. It forms as winds blow away fine-grained surficial sediments, leaving coarser particles, such as pieces of gravel, behind. As the fine sediments are deposited elsewhere, they work their way between and underneath larger particles. Rain events, though infrequent, provide water that causes particles of clay to expand. As the water evaporates, the clays dry and shrink. These cycles of expansion and shrinkage promote the uplift of coarser particles to the surface. After a desert pavement develops, it shields underlying sediments from further erosion by winds or water.

Deposits of sand in deserts often form wind-sculpted, shifting ridges called **dunes**. When dunes cover an extensive area, the type of desert formed is known as an **erg desert**.

Wind

The horizontal motion of air over Earth's surface is called **wind**. Wind erosion tends to dominate in deserts, primarily due to the lack of water, even though the density of air is much lower than that of water or ice. The two main types of wind erosion in deserts are deflation and abrasion. **Deflation** occurs as loose particles are blown away by wind, gradually lowering the land surface. The process of abrasion involves the "sandblasting" of exposed rock surfaces by eolian particles. **Eolian** (also spelled **aeolian**) materials are those that have been eroded, transported, and deposited by winds.

Eolian abrasion causes rock surfaces to have a pitted, grooved, or polished appearance. Rocks that have experienced a large amount of abrasion generally have an aerodynamic shape oriented according to the direction of the prevailing winds. Such rocks are called **ventifacts**. When deflation and abrasion operate on large outcrops of rock, they can create streamlined, elongated structures parallel to the direction of the prevailing wind, which are called **yardangs**. These structures can be kilometers long and many meters high.

Dunes

Sand dunes form as windblown sand grains are deposited, and their continued erosion and deposition causes them to migrate across a desert. Winds push grains upslope on the side of a dune facing the wind, and grains tumble down the leeward side, also called a **slipface**.

Dune forms can be grouped into three major classes—crescentic, linear, and star dunes. A **crescentic dune**, or **barchan dune**, is the most common type. It has the shape of a crescent moon or is U-shaped, with ends that point in the direction that the wind blows. This type of dune forms when the wind blows predominantly from one direction. A **linear dune** has a straighter shape than a crescentic dune and has a well-defined ridge. This type of dune can extend long distances and tends to form in sets of parallel dunes. A **star dune** has ridges that come together to form a central peak, making a shape similar to that of a pinwheel. It forms where wind patterns are constantly changing, so it has multiple slipfaces. Star dunes can grow quite tall.

Hydrologic Cycle

Water is present on Earth in the atmosphere, on the planet's surface, and in its near-surface rocks. It can be a liquid, solid (ice), or gas (water vapor). It can be fresh or saline.

The movement of water among its various reservoirs, and in its various forms, is summarized in a generalized model called the **water cycle**, or the **hydrologic cycle**. Most of Earth's water (more than ninety-seven percent) is contained in the ocean that covers the majority of the planet's surface. Therefore, it is the site of the bulk of the **evaporation** that adds water vapor to the atmosphere and **precipitation** that returns water to the surface in the form of rain or ice crystals. Some of the water evaporated from the ocean is transferred by **advection**, or lateral transport, through the atmosphere to land areas, where it falls as precipitation. On land, much of the water in soils returns to the atmosphere through the process of **evapotranspiration**, which involves the uptake of water by plant roots and its migration to leaves, where it is released as water vapor. Water that infiltrates into the ground and reaches the water table becomes **groundwater**.

Most of Earth's freshwater is contained as ice in glaciers. The second-largest amount is groundwater. Only a small percentage is present at any one time in the atmosphere or in streams and lakes, even though water constantly cycles among these reservoirs.

TECTONIC EARTH PROCESSES

This section of the subject review covers tectonic Earth processes, including weathering, mass wasting, streams, floods, groundwater, glaciers and glaciation, oceanic and coastal systems, deserts, wind, and the hydrologic cycle. Questions on this topic account for 30 percent of the DSST exam.

Geologic Time

Planetary Geology

Planetary geology involves applying geological principles and concepts to study celestial bodies (such as planets other than Earth, moons, asteroids, and comets) using data collected by remote-sensing instruments and the exploration of Earth's moon (and other planets and their moons) by human expeditions or robotic devices. A partial list of topics in planetary science includes the investigation of the following:

- Surface conditions and internal structure of the **terrestrial planets** (also called the **rocky planets**) of the inner solar system—Mercury, Venus, Earth, and Mars—and their moons
- Composition and structure of the **gas giant planets** of the outer solar system—Jupiter, Saturn, Neptune, and Uranus—and their moons
- Occurrence and effects of meteorite impacts
- Origin, history, and properties of
  - extraterrestrial objects, such as meteorites, that have reached Earth
  - asteroids, comets, and Kuiper Belt objects
  - **extrasolar planets** (planets not in our solar system)

Planetary geology also involves the investigation of our solar system. According to the **nebular hypothesis**, the solar system originated from a cloud of gases—mainly hydrogen and helium—and scattered dust grains. This cloud, called a **nebula**, had a low temperature and low density. The force of gravity acted to pull the cloud together, and about 4.5 billion years ago, the solar system formed.

As the central part of the nebula underwent a gravitational collapse, its temperature and density greatly increased. A young star called a **protostar** formed. When conditions in the protostar became right for hydrogen to efficiently participate in nuclear fusion reactions, the protostar became a full-fledged star: the sun.

The sun contains most of the mass that was present in the nebula. The remaining materials formed a disk around the sun, in which the **accretion** (coming together) of dust grains formed small bodies called **planetesimals**. The higher temperatures closer to the sun promoted the formation of rocky planetesimals, while the cooler temperatures in the outer part of the disk led to the formation of icy planetesimals. The accretion of planetesimals resulted in the formation of the planets and their moons. Leftover planetesimals became **asteroids** and **comets**.

Relative Time

A **relative time scale** describes the order in which events happened but does not assign precise dates to those events. For instance, we can say that the sun formed before Earth and its moon did, without saying how many billions of years ago each event occurred.

Geologists often use the concept of relative time to describe the sequence of events that has shaped an area, such as when rock strata formed. This technique is called **relative dating**. By observing the relative positions of strata, geologists can identify lower layers as being older, and higher layers being younger. This technique is most appropriate for use in strata that have not been overly disturbed by tectonic processes and strata that have not had an igneous intrusion inject younger layers between older ones.

The study of the rock layers in an area, including how they have been formed and changed by geologic processes, is called **stratigraphy**. A **stratigraphic succession** puts the layers and geological events in order by age, even when the actual ages are unknown. Determining a stratigraphic succession is particularly useful for analyzing the history of layers of sedimentary rock. The nature of sedimentary deposition causes layers to be built up in order, from bottom to top.

A subset of stratigraphic succession is **fossil succession**, by which scientists compare the relative ages of fossils found in different layers of rock in the same area. They can then use this information to help decipher the history of other areas in which some of these fossils occur.

Absolute Time

The **geologic time scale** relates both relative time and absolute time to events on Earth throughout its history. In geology, **absolute time** is determined when it is possible to assign a date in years before present to an event, such as the formation of a body of rock, occurrence of regional metamorphism, or emplacement of an igneous intrusion. The geologic time scale is divided into long intervals called **eons**. In turn, eons are divided into **eras**; eras are divided into **periods**; periods are divided into **epochs**; and epochs are divided into **ages**. Each of these intervals have start and end dates, usually expressed in terms of millions or billions of years ago.

Absolute ages are determined by analyzing radioactive isotopes incorporated into rocks. **Isotopes** are atoms of an element that contain different numbers of neutrons in their nucleus. A radioactive isotope changes, or decays, into another isotope according to its characteristic **half-life**—the amount of time required for half of its atoms to decay into a daughter isotope. **Isotopic dating**, also called **radiometric dating**, involves measuring the relative amounts of a radioactive isotope and its daughter isotope present in a rock. For example, uranium-238 decays into lead-206 with a half-life of 4.5 billion years, so determining the amount of each isotope allows the calculation of the number of half-lives that have elapsed since the uranium-containing minerals formed. The uranium-238 system can be used to date ancient rocks. Radioactive isotopes with shorter half-lives are suitable for determining the ages of younger rocks.

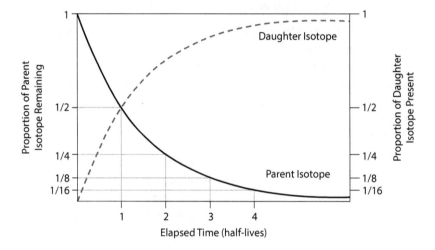

Figure 5: Amount of Radioactive Isotope Remaining after Successive Half-Lives

Field Relations

Layers of related or interlayered rock types that are distinct from surrounding layers make up a geologic **formation**. A formation must have sufficient thickness and extent to be plotted on a geologic map. A set of formations makes up a **group**. Subdivisions of a formation are called **members**. Members contain **beds**, which are the smallest subdivisions of a formation.

No matter whether geologists are dealing with groups of formations or a series of individual beds, they apply the **principle of superposition**, which states that layers of undisturbed rocks and sediments are always arranged with the youngest beds near and at the top of a sequence and the oldest at the base.

Geologists also rely on the principle of uniformitarianism when analyzing the stratigraphic record. **Uniformitarianism** is often expressed as "the present is the key to the past," meaning that the geologic processes acting today are the same that have been acting throughout geologic time. Therefore, for example, a mafic magma that erupts as lava at Earth's surface cools to form basalt, whether the eruption occurred last week or billions of years ago.

Although geologic time is generally characterized by processes that slowly shape and reshape the landscape, some dramatic, large-scale events occur rapidly. Such events include asteroid impacts, massive earthquakes, and huge landslides. Therefore, within uniformitarianism is the concept of **punctuated equilibrium**, in which the usual flow of events is briefly interrupted by quick changes and then resumes.

Structural Geology

Structural geology is the study of processes that cause rock deformation and the effects of these processes. Unraveling the history of deformation in an area involves identification of changes in local and regional processes related to movement of rock in the crust. Geologic structures are usually produced by forces related to the movement of tectonic plates. Plate movements lead to such events as the formation of faults and large-scale folds as well as the uplift of mountains. In areas where multiple deformational events have occurred, such as when new faulting occurs in already faulted rock or when already folded rock is folded again, geologic structures can become quite complex.

Plate boundaries are dynamic locations, as shown by the prevalence of earthquake and volcanic activity occurring along them. Along divergent boundaries, which are often characterized by seafloor spreading centers, **tensional forces** predominate. Convergent boundaries, which occur where oceanic–oceanic, oceanic–continental, or continental–continental plates collide, are dominated by **compressive forces**. Transform boundaries, along which plates slide laterally past one another, are dominated by **shearing forces**.

Folding

Folds form when rocks subjected to compressive forces bend in a **ductile** manner (called **plastic deformation**) rather than break in a brittle manner. Therefore, folds form deep in the crust where rocks are warm enough to experience plastic deformation. Various conditions, such as the following, must be met for folding to take place.

- The process of deformation must occur slowly in order for the rock to have time to bend instead of fracturing.
- Pressure and temperature must be high enough to promote ductile behavior.
- Pressure must not be too high because if it is greater than the rocks' internal strength, the rocks will fracture instead of bending.

Geologists classify a simple fold as being a monocline, syncline, or anticline, shown in the following figure.

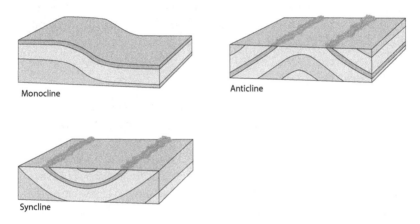

Figure 6: Basic Fold Types

A **monocline** is characterized by a single bend in rock layers. In a **syncline**, layers of rock resemble a nested set of bowls, and the youngest rock is in the center. The sides, or **limbs**, of the fold dip toward the center, or **hinge**, of the fold. In an **anticline**, rock layers form an arch, and the oldest rock is in the center. Its limbs dip away from its hinge. More intricate folds can develop when an area has a complex deformational history. Synclines and anticlines can become tilted and asymmetrical and may become **recumbent** (i.e., turned onto one side) or even completely overturned.

Faulting

A **fault** forms when rocks fracture and move past one another in a process called **faulting**. Movement along a fault often occurs as a sudden release of energy that produces an earthquake. (Very slow movement, or **creep**, can also occur along a fault.)

Types of faults are named according to the way the blocks of rock move relative to one another along the **fault plane**—the fracture surface along which movement occurs.

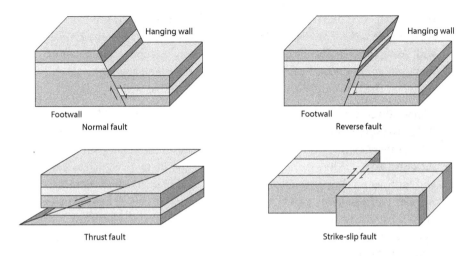

Figure 7: Basic Fault Types

Tensional forces result in the formation of **normal faults**. In this type of fault, the **footwall**, located below the fault plane, moves down relative to the **hanging wall**, which is located above the fault plane. Compressive forces result in the formation of **reverse faults**, characterized by the movement of the hanging wall upward relative to the footwall. A low-angle reverse fault is called a **thrust fault**. Shearing forces result in the formation of **strike-slip faults**, also called **transform faults**. This type of fault has a vertical fault plane, and the blocks of rock move horizontally past one another.

Mountain Building

A mountain-building episode, an **orogeny**, results in the formation of mountains as a result of large-scale deformation that causes the folding, faulting, and thickening of crustal rock. Major orogenies occur along convergent and divergent tectonic plate boundaries.

Along an oceanic–continental convergent boundary, compressive forces cause **folded mountains** to form, and subduction of the oceanic plate leads to the generation of magma that can rise through the overlying continental plate and erupt through volcanoes. The magma can also cool within the crust to produce large bodies of igneous rock called **plutons**. An example is the Andes mountain chain along the west coast of South America, which is the result of the subduction of the Nazca Plate under the South American Plate. Along a continental–continental collision boundary, continental crust undergoes folding and thickening, but no volcanism. An example is the Himalayan Mountains, a result of the collision of India with Asia. The collision of two oceanic plates leads to subduction of one of them, which results in the formation of a volcanic island arc on the overlying plate. The islands of the Philippines are an example.

Along a divergent boundary in the ocean, such as the Atlantic Mid-Ocean Ridge, the submarine mountain ranges that make up Earth's mid-ocean ridge system form as heat from rising magma causes thermal inflation of the crust. Along a divergent boundary under a continent, tensional forces and continental rifting results in the formation of **fault-block mountains**. As their name suggests, this type of mountain range forms as huge blocks of rock are tilted along faults, causing one side to lift up and the other side to sink down. The tall mountains located along the East African Rift Valley are fault-block mountains. Extensive volcanism is also present in the rift system.

Volcanoes and Volcanic Hazards

An opening through which lava erupts is called a **volcano**. Volcanoes are located along tectonic plate boundaries at which subduction or rifting is occurring and over **hotspots**—areas where a plume of particularly hot mantle material rises, promoting volcanism at the surface.

Repeated eruptions of volcanic materials can build up a mountain over time that is also called a volcano. At the summit of a volcano is a roughly circular depression called a **crater**, from which volcanic materials emerge during an eruption. Under a volcano, magma rises and collects in an area called a **magma chamber**. When conditions are right, an eruption occurs, and magma rises through conduits in the volcano and erupts. A volcanic eruption can take place at side vents as well as at the main crater. If an eruption is large enough to partially empty the magma chamber, the suddenly unsupported top of the volcano can collapse, forming a large, roughly circular basin called a **caldera**. Although a volcano can be a huge mountain, it can also be a much smaller, less dramatic structure, such as a cinder cone.

Types of Volcanoes and Volcanic Eruptions

The four main types of volcanoes are (1) shield, (2) cinder cone, (3) lava dome, and (4) composite volcanoes, also called stratovolcanoes.

Shield volcanoes get their name from their shape, similar to the profile of a curved warrior's shield lying right side up on the ground. Their low, mounded form develops because they produce large amounts of low-viscosity basaltic lava that is capable of flowing long distances. As lava from each eruption cools, another layer of rock is added to the structure. Shield volcanoes are common at divergent boundaries and volcanic hotspots. Examples of shield volcanoes include Mount Kilauea and Mauna Loa on the big island of Hawaii, which overlies a hotspot.

Shield volcanoes commonly experience **effusive eruptions** in which large volumes of lava flow out onto and over the ground. These eruptions are considered relatively gentle, which means they are nonexplosive, although they can produce spectacular lava fountains when rapidly escaping gases carry pieces of fragmented lava into the air before they fall back to the ground.

At the other extreme from massive shield volcanoes are the small **cinder cone volcanoes**. Their structure is simple—they possess small, conical hills built of pieces of hardened lava called **cinders**. When a cinder cone erupts, gas-rich lava is fragmented, and pieces of lava thrown into the air cool and solidify as they descend. These cinders accumulate around the single, central vent, building up the volcanic edifice.

Lava domes form from high-viscosity lava whose "stickiness" largely hinders its ability to flow. Therefore, the lava accumulates in bulbous piles over or near its vent. A lava dome tends to grow by expansion as new lava is injected into its interior. Lava domes are common in the craters and at the side vents of composite volcanoes.

Composite volcanoes, or **stratovolcanoes**, are common along convergent boundaries where subduction is occurring. They grow to form tall, cone-shaped mountains. This type of volcano experiences **explosive eruptions** because its lava is more silica-rich, and hence more viscous, than lava involved in effusive eruptions. Its higher viscosity makes it "sticky" and much more likely to harden into plugs within volcanic conduits. The plugs block the flow of additional lava and allow internal pressure from rising magma, and the gases trying to escape from it, to build inside the volcano. When the pressure becomes high enough, the volcano erupts explosively. Composite volcanoes get their name because they are built up of accumulations of solid volcanic debris ejected during eruptions that are interlayered with viscous flows of lava that cannot travel far before they cool.

Volcanic Hazards

The effusive eruptions commonly produced by shield volcanoes may result in extensive lava flows that cover ecosystems and destroy property, but they rarely cause injury or death to humans. The limited extent of cinder cone or lava dome eruptions mitigate their hazards. However, the explosive eruptions produced by composite volcanoes pose myriad dangers to humans and property.

Hazards accompanying volcanic activity include the following:

- Ejection of **tephra** or **pyroclastic** particles of rock and debris that range in size from potentially massive chunks (**volcanic bombs**) to tiny fragments of rock (**volcanic ash**)
- **Lahar** debris flows in which particles of rocks of all sizes mix with water on a volcano, commonly produced by the flash-melting of snow and ice at and near the summit by the heat of an eruption
- **Pyroclastic flows** (superheated mixtures of gases and pyroclastic debris) with densities high enough to cause the flows to hug the ground as they race downslope
- Landslides and avalanches on steep volcanic slopes
- **Lava flows** that generally travel slow enough for humans to escape but can engulf landscapes
- Release of **volcanic gases**, including carbon dioxide, that can displace air, and sulfur-containing compounds that can combine with water in air to form sulfuric acid
- **Tsunamis** created by the eruption of an underwater volcano or an eruption-triggered landslide that cascades into the ocean

Hazards typically associated with effusive eruptions include extensive lava flows and the release of gases that can form acids capable of chemically burning vegetation and causing severe eye and lung irritation. Although composite volcanoes are unlikely to produce widespread lava flows, they may emit dangerous gases. Explosive eruptions can throw volcanic bombs for kilometers, and volcanic ash contained in eruption columns towering into the sky can be transported hundreds or thousands of kilometers by winds before it settles back to the ground. Thick accumulations of ash can smother crops and cause roofs to collapse. The engines of airplanes that fly into ash clouds may fail as they become clogged with ash. Lahars have the consistency of wet concrete and can flow long distances, typically following stream channels and valleys. Pyroclastic flows race down the slopes of a volcano at tremendous speeds, burning or burying everything in their path. The ancient city of **Pompeii** was buried by pyroclastic flows.

Fast-moving tsunami waves can travel across the ocean and cause seawater to inundate distant shorelines. Tsunamis, which can also be generated by earthquakes, can cause catastrophic damage.

Geophysics

Earthquakes and Seismology

An **earthquake** is produced by the sudden movement of blocks of rock along a fault. Energy from an earthquake is released as **seismic waves** that travel within Earth. The study of earthquakes and seismic waves is known as **seismology**.

The point on a fault plane where movement first occurs during an earthquake is called the **focus**, or **hypocenter**. Seismic waves produced by an earthquake move outward in all directions from the focus. The point on Earth's surface directly above the focus is called the **epicenter**. An earthquake may be preceded in the same general area by a weaker earthquake, called a **foreshock**, or followed by an **aftershock**.

The **elastic-rebound theory** describes why earthquakes occur. According to this theory, the blocks of rock on either side of a fault are locked together by friction. Slow movements in nearby rock, like those caused by the shifting of tectonic plates, cause stress and strain to build up along the fault, deforming the adjacent rock and storing increasing amounts of energy in it. Localized areas of high strain along a fault are called **asperities**. These areas break loose when the accumulated strain overcomes the frictional forces, allowing an earthquake to occur. The accumulated energy is released in the form of seismic waves, and the deformed rock on either side of the fault snaps back, or rebounds, into its original configuration.

Seismic energy travels through Earth as two types of **body waves**: (1) primary, or **P waves**, and (2) secondary, or **S waves**. P waves are compressional waves that can travel through solid or molten rock. S waves are shear waves that can travel only through solid rock. P waves travel faster than S waves. When seismic waves reach Earth's surface, they can travel along it as **surface waves**, which are responsible for earthquake-caused damage and devastation to buildings and other human-made structures.

Seismic waves are recorded at seismic stations by devices called **seismographs**. The difference in arrival times of P waves and S waves as recorded by a seismograph is used to calculate how far away an earthquake was. Data from at least three seismic stations are needed to triangulate the earthquake's location.

The strength of an earthquake can be assessed according to various scales: the older Richter scale, the more modern and accurate moment-magnitude scale, and the descriptive Mercalli scale. The **Richter scale**, developed by Charles Richter, is a logarithmic scale in which an increase by one whole number represents a ten-fold increase in the amplitude of seismic waves recorded by a seismograph. This increase in number on the scale translates into about a 32-fold increase in the amount of energy released by the earthquake. The Richter scale has shortcomings, such as not being able to properly quantify the magnitude of the most powerful earthquakes. Most seismologists now use the **moment-magnitude scale**, which is also a logarithmic scale. It is more accurate because it also considers the amount of movement that occurs along a fault, the areal extent of the subsurface rupture, and the resistance of the rock along the fault to movement. Magnitudes measured on both scales are quite similar for earthquakes of low to medium intensity, but the moment-magnitude scale is much more accurate for high-intensity earthquakes.

Unlike the Richter or moment-magnitude scale that produce a single numeric value to describe an earthquake's intensity, the values assigned according to the **Mercalli scale** vary from location to location. This measurement system uses Roman numerals, ranging from I to XII, to represent descriptions of intensity from "barely felt" to "catastrophic total destruction." Maps showing Mercalli scale ratings of damage caused by previous earthquakes are particularly useful when developing construction standards for earthquake-prone areas because the degree of shaking experienced during an earthquake varies in part according to the nature of the subsurface underlying an area.

Our present knowledge of seismology does not allow for the prediction of any particular earthquake. Instead, **earthquake probabilities** are determined, in part, by assessing the frequency and intensity of past earthquakes in an area. The accumulated strain in rock along a fault can also be measured. An area of high strain that is overdue for an earthquake is called a **seismic gap**. All of this information goes into producing earthquake probabilities, which take the form of a statement such as "There is a 40-percent probability of a magnitude 7 or higher earthquake occurring within 50 kilometers of a particular location within the next 30 years." Earthquake probabilities are used to produce seismic hazard maps.

Earth's Interior

Scientists have learned a great deal about Earth's internal structure by studying the paths and behavior of seismic waves. Seismic waves can reflect, or bounce off, boundaries between layers with different properties, and their travel speeds vary according to the nature of the material they are passing through. P waves can propagate through both solid and molten rock, but S waves are absorbed by molten rock. These variations allow geophysicists to analyze the properties of the planet's layers.

At the surface of Earth is the cool rock of the **crust**. The two types of crust are (1) **oceanic crust** composed of basalt, a rock rich in mafic minerals, and (2) **continental crust** with a predominantly granitic composition, indicating that felsic minerals are abundant. Oceanic crust has an average density of 3.0 g/cm^3, whereas continental crust has an average density of 2.7 g/cm^3. The **mantle** is directly below the crust. The crust and the cool rock of the uppermost part of the mantle form the **lithosphere**, which is broken into huge, slowly moving tectonic plates.

The boundary between the crust and the uppermost mantle is called the **Mohorovičić discontinuity**, or **Moho** for short. It is named for the seismologist who discovered that the travel speeds of seismic waves change abruptly at this boundary as a result of the greater density of mantle rock.

The portion of the upper mantle immediately below the lithosphere is called the **asthenosphere**. In this layer, temperatures are high enough and pressures are low enough to allow convection of mantle rock to occur, even though the rock is still mostly solid. Its behavior is said to be plastic because of its ability to deform and flow with relative ease. These convection currents allow the overlying tectonic plates to move. The average density of the asthenosphere is 3.3 g/cm^3.

The lower mantle is below the asthenosphere. It is hotter but denser than the asthenosphere. Convection and other dynamics in the lower mantle are topics of ongoing research. Density in the mantle increases with depth to about 5.6 g/cm^3. Below the lower mantle is Earth's **outer core**. The boundary between these regions is rough and uneven, forming a transition zone several hundred kilometers thick called the **Gutenberg discontinuity**. The outer core is known to be molten because S waves cannot travel through it. This creates **shadow zones** on opposite sides of Earth from where an earthquake occurs in which no S waves from the earthquake can be detected. The composition of the outer core (density: 9.9 to 12.2 g/cm^3) and **inner core** (density: 12.6 to 13.0 g/cm^3) is the same: mostly an iron–nickel alloy, with some other dense elements mixed in. The inner core is hotter than the outer core but is solid because of the high pressures at Earth's center. The dynamics in the core generate Earth's magnetic field.

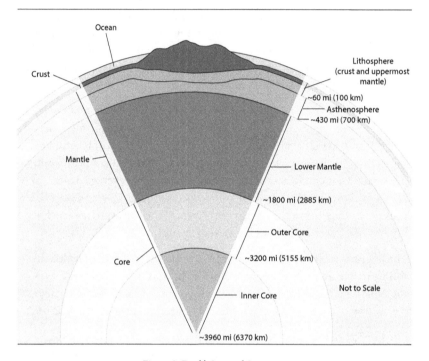

Figure 8: Earth's Internal Structure

Gravity and Isostasy

Lithospheric plates are less dense than the underlying asthenosphere, so they can be considered to "float" on it, even though the asthenosphere is mostly solid. Portions of the lithosphere that are heavier, such as regions with mountain ranges or continental glaciers, sink deeper into the asthenosphere. Regions of lower density float higher. This equilibrium between buoyancy and gravity is called **isostasy**. Because geologic processes are slowly but constantly causing large-scale changes to Earth's surface, slow **isostatic adjustments** are constantly taking place. For example, in regions where thick glacial ice from the last ice age has melted away, the land is adjusting by rising, a process called **glacial rebound**. Regions where thick loads of sediment are accumulating, or where mountains are forming, are sinking lower.

APPLICATIONS

The applications section of the DSST covers mineral and energy resources, environmental geology, and climate change. Questions on this topic account for 10 percent of the DSST exam.

Mineral and Energy Resources

Mineral Resources

A body of rock that contains useful elements or minerals in a high enough concentration to be economically mined is called an **ore**. An ore can form in various ways. For example, extensive evaporation of mineral-rich water at Earth's surface can lead to the deposition of halite (salt), which is used in food, or gypsum, which is used in the manufacturing of plaster. Certain clay minerals are important for the making of pottery or to coat paper.

Processes related to igneous intrusions or contact metamorphism are important in the formation of many types of valuable ores. These processes promote the circulation of hydrothermal fluids that can dissolve minerals from one location and deposit them in another. Many metal ores are formed when rock becomes enriched with metals through the precipitation of minerals. Deposition can be widely disseminated throughout a body of rock, producing fairly low concentrations of the desired minerals, or can be concentrated in fractures to form rich veins of ore.

Mineral deposits form on the seafloor at **hydrothermal vents**, which are associated with mid-ocean ridge systems. Hot water rich in dissolved minerals emerge from the vents and immediately encounter the cold temperatures of the water in the deep ocean. The sudden chilling of the hydrothermal solution causes minerals to precipitate around the vents. Tectonic processes can carry these deposits toward collision zones, where some of them may be scraped off the subducting oceanic plate and added to the edge of a continent. Ancient deposits formed in this way are mined on land, but it is not yet economically feasible to directly mine currently forming hydrothermal vent deposits on the seafloor.

Sand, Gravel, and Rock Resources

Deposits of sand and gravel are mined for use in making concrete for buildings and roads. Rock or other hard material that is mixed with a cementing material to produce mortar, plaster, or concrete is called **aggregate**. In areas where gravel deposits are not readily available, crushed rock is used as aggregate. In addition to its use in construction, aggregate can also be used to absorb wave energy along a coastline, reducing erosion. Deposits of relatively pure sands that have a high quartz content are used in the manufacture of glass.

Minerals such as marble, granite, and limestone are used as construction materials. Marble in particular is used for decorative purposes in buildings and for sculptures.

Energy Resources

Coal, oil, and natural gas, collectively known as **fossil fuels**, are the primary sources of energy used for industrial and household needs. Fossil fuels form over millions of years from accumulations of the remains of once-living organisms. Because they take so long to form, they are **finite resources**. When they are burned, they release gases that can affect climate.

Coal forms when large accumulations of plant matter partially decay and then are buried by subsequent layers of sediments. The increase in heat and pressure associated with burial transforms the plant matter into coal. The three main types of coal are (1) **lignite**, which has a relatively low carbon content and a low heating value, (2) **bituminous** coal, which has a higher carbon content and heating value, and (3) **anthracite**, which has the highest carbon content and heating value. Coal is mainly used for the generation of electricity in coal-burning power plants. **Anthracite**, because it burns more cleanly than other types of coal, may be used to heat homes.

Natural gas is primarily composed of methane. It forms mainly from the remains of ancient marine microorganisms. Additional sediments deposited on top of these organic remains cut off the oxygen supply and subject them to increasing amounts of heat and pressure that over millions of years converted them into compounds of carbon and hydrogen called **hydrocarbons**. The amount of heat and pressure largely determines whether natural gas or oil forms. Small hydrocarbon molecules, such as methane, are gases. Along with coal, natural gas is used to generate electricity. It is also used for heating and as a transportation fuel, primarily by bus fleets. Natural gas burns more cleanly than coal or oil, producing almost no sulfur dioxide emissions and much smaller emissions of nitrogen oxide and particulates. These substances are pollutants, and some of them can affect climate.

Oil is a mixture of liquid hydrocarbons that are larger and more complex than the hydrocarbons in natural gas. Oil is widely used as a transportation fuel. It forms in a similar manner as natural gas, but under different conditions of heat and pressure. It is generally pumped from underground reservoirs. Although much of the retrieved oil is processed to make gasoline, it is also used for many other purposes, such as the manufacture of plastics.

Environmental Geology

Environmental geology is concerned with interactions between humans and the geologic environment. Human activities affect and are affected by processes involving rocks, soil, water, and air. Environmental geology calls on knowledge and techniques from all branches of geology, including stratigraphy, structural geology, and hydrology, to identify and, to the extent possible, remediate environmental problems such as the following:

- **Geologic hazards**, including mass wasting events, volcanic eruptions, and earthquakes
- **Waste management and storage**, including the siting and maintenance of landfills to protect supplies of clean water
- **Extraction of natural resources**, including mining ores and pumping oil from underground

Environmental geologists collect, synthesize, and present information in ways that are useful for policymakers and the general public. Their activities include evaluating the risk of and potential for damage by events such as floods, lava flows, or sinkhole collapse. One of the ways they present this information is by producing **environmental hazard maps**. In addition, environmental geologists are often involved in such decisions as the suitable uses for a parcel of land or where to drill wells to tap into groundwater resources.

Climate Change

Weather describes the atmospheric conditions present at a location at a given moment in time. It can change from minute to minute. **Climate** describes average conditions for an area, including such natural variations as the frequency of intense rain events, heat waves, and cold snaps, over the course of decades. The study of climate is called **climatology**. Key components of climate include patterns include the following:

- **Insolation**: the amount of solar radiation received at Earth's surface, which varies with day length, latitude, season, and amount and duration of cloud cover
- **Temperature**: varies with insolation, altitude, and proximity to large bodies of water
- **Precipitation**: (e.g., rain, sleet, snow, and hail) varies with atmospheric moisture content, temperature, and types of clouds present
- **Air pressure**: measure of the weight of the atmosphere above a particular location
- **Movement of air masses**: driven by changes in air pressure

Tools used by climatologists include sophisticated computer models that simulate the interactions among the different parts of Earth's system that contribute to climate.

Paleoclimatology

The study of past climates is called **paleoclimatology**. By understanding past climatic conditions, how and why they changed, and how rapidly they changed, we can better understand and plan for current and future changes in climate. Paleoclimatology also provides data used to test the accuracy of climate models—the more accurately the models reproduce past known climate conditions, the more confidence we can put in them.

Earth's climate has historically experienced intervals of warmer or cooler temperatures. Extended episodes of generally cold climatic conditions are called **ice ages**. During an ice age, temperatures do not remain uniformly cold. Instead, during **glacial** colder intervals, the area covered by ice and snow expands. During **interglacial** warmer intervals, the ice and snow retreat. As ice advances during a glacial period, it bulldozes over evidence of prior advances, making the glacial record on land more complex to interpret. Some of the best evidence for the timing of glacial and interglacial intervals is recorded in accumulations of oceanic sediment. Fossils of tiny marine organisms present vary with the temperature of water at and near the surface, and bulk sediment properties also commonly change from glacial to interglacial intervals.

The causes of an ice age include a complex mix of interacting variables, such as the location of continents and the configuration of ocean basins, and astronomical factors such as Milankovitch cycles. There are three such interacting cycles: (1) eccentricity, (2) axial tilt, and (3) precession. **Eccentricity** describes changes in Earth's orbit from more circular to more elliptical, and back again, which occurs in roughly 100,000-year cycles. **Axial tilt** describes the amount of tilt of Earth's axis, which varies between about 22.1° and 24.5° on about a 40,000-year cycle. **Precession** describes the "wobble" of Earth's axis, which can be compared to the wobble of a spinning toy top. A precession cycle takes about 26,000 years. In combination, these three cycles affect the distribution of insolation at Earth's surface, and therefore heating patterns and climate.

Ice cores collected from thick glaciers aid in the study of climate because they contain evidence of the chemical and physical properties of the atmosphere at the time snow fell and was transformed into glacial ice. These cores contain air bubbles that are samples of the atmosphere when compression cut off exchange of gases with the air. Therefore, analysis of these bubbles allows the determination of past atmospheric concentrations of climatically important gases such as carbon dioxide and methane. In addition, high concentrations of wind-blown dust mark times of widespread cold and dry conditions, and volcanic ash incorporated into the ice allows for radiometric dating, which provides a timeline.

Earth's Changing Climate

A major factor influencing the temperature of the atmosphere and surface of Earth is the **greenhouse effect**. Consider how a greenhouse is used to grow plants. Transparent glass allows sunlight to pass through. As the sunlight is absorbed by surfaces in the greenhouse, the shorter wavelengths of visible light are transformed into longer wavelengths of infrared radiation and radiated back into the air. The glass, which is not transparent to infrared energy, traps some of the energy as heat, preventing the heated air from mixing with the surrounding atmosphere.

In the atmosphere, the greenhouse effect is due to the presence of radiatively active gases, called **greenhouse gases**, that are transparent in incoming short-wavelength solar radiation, but absorb and reradiate energy at the longer wavelengths of the outgoing infrared radiation released from

Earth's surface. This outgoing radiation is not trapped in the atmosphere. Instead, its repeated absorption and re-radiation delays its escape to space, thereby warming Earth's surface and the air in contact with it. The greenhouse effect is a natural effect that raises temperatures and allows liquid water to be present over much of the planet.

The **enhanced greenhouse effect** that is caused by the addition of more greenhouse gases to the atmosphere is a matter of grave concern. Most of the **anthropogenic**, or human-caused, increase in greenhouse gases is due to the burning of fossil fuels. As the concentrations of radiatively active gases such as carbon dioxide increase in the atmosphere, Earth's surface and near surface become progressively warmer. Although this is sometimes referred to as **global warming**, a better term is **global climate change** because increased energy in the atmosphere causes changes in moisture and precipitation patterns as well as in temperature.

Ice core data show that the modern-day concentration of atmospheric greenhouse gases has climbed at a much faster rate than natural variations that have occurred in connection to glacial and interglacial intervals. Climatic changes, therefore, may occur faster than ecosystems can adapt, leading to widespread disruptions.

SUMMING IT UP

- **Geology** is the study of the physical structures and substances that make up Earth.
- **Minerals** are inorganic solids with definite chemical compositions, physical properties, and regular, repeating crystalline structures.
- Minerals are classified into **families**, the largest of which is the **silicate family**. In descending order, the families are **silicate, carbonate, sulfate, sulfide, halide,** and **oxide.** Native element minerals contain only one element, such as gold or copper.
- **Felsic minerals** are primarily made up of feldspar and silica. They are less dense than mafic minerals.
- **Mafic minerals** are primarily made up of magnesium and iron and are more dense than felsic minerals.
- **Rocks** are made up of minerals or, on occasion, just one mineral. There are three groups of rocks: **igneous, sedimentary,** and **metamorphic.**
- **Igneous rocks** are formed by the cooling of molten rock, either from underground (magma) or on the surface (lava).
    - ◉ **Intrusive igneous rocks** are formed by magma that is lower in density than the rock surrounding it, causing it to push into and through the rock. Intrusive igneous rock cools slowly, resulting in coarse grains visible without magnification. Granite and gabbro are common intrusive igneous rocks.
    - ◉ **Extrusive igneous rock** is formed by lava on the surface. It cools quickly, resulting in fine-grained rock. Obsidian, basalt, and pumice are examples of extrusive igneous rock.
- **Sedimentary rocks** are made up from pieces of other rocks that have broken off and been subsequently pressed together. Sedimentary rock can also be made up of organic materials such as shells and plant matter.
- **Metamorphic rocks** are formed from igneous or sedimentary rock that has been recrystallized by heat, pressure, or chemically active fluids.
- The **rock cycle** shows the processes rocks undergo over time. Rocks can form, break apart, re-form, melt, cool, and be metamorphosed. Rocks do not follow a pattern through the rock cycle; that is, they can break apart, melt, extrude, cool, break apart, erode, or change under pressure at random.
- Earth is made up of layers of solid rock and magma. The outer layer is the **crust;** the two types of crust are the **continental crust** and **oceanic crust.** Below this is the **mantle,** divided into the upper **mantle,** the **asthenosphere,** and the **lower mantle.** The crust and upper mantle make up the **lithosphere.** Below the lower mantle is the **outer and inner core.**

- **Plate tectonics** is the study of the movement of huge plates that make up the lithosphere. Tectonic plates move slowly (centimeters per year), interacting with other tectonic plates and causing rock to deform and fold, pushing up mountain ranges and causing earthquakes and volcanic activity. **Plate boundaries** are zones where two or more plates meet. Plates interact by pushing together, pulling apart, or sliding past one another.
- Tectonic plates contain continental crust (which is less dense), oceanic crust (more dense), or both. A **subduction zone** is where an oceanic plate sinks below a continental plate, while a **seafloor spreading center** is where oceanic plates pull apart, allowing the formation of new oceanic crust.
- **Geophysics** is the study of seismology, or earthquakes and seismic waves. The two types of seismic waves are fast-moving primary **P waves**, and slower secondary **S waves**. P waves can travel through solid rock as well as magma, while S waves are limited to solid rock. When seismic waves reach the surface, they become surface waves that cause damage to manufactured structures.
- **Geomagnetics** is the study of the effect of Earth's magnetic field on iron-rich mafic minerals.
- **Weathering** is a process that breaks rocks into smaller pieces (**mechanical weathering**) or dissolves them in water (**chemical weathering**).
- **Soil** is made up of organic material, minerals, water, and air. The thickness of soil from the surface to the lowest point plants can reach is called the soil profile. The soil profile is made up of layers, called **horizons**. Typically, a soil profile has five horizons: O, A, E, B, and C.
- **Mass wasting** events occur when gravity causes surface material to move down a slope. There are four classifications of mass wasting events: **falls**, **slides**, **flows**, and **creep**.
- Regardless of size or volume, any moving body of water is a **stream**. Streams occupy drainage basins, which are places such as lakes or rivers where precipitation collects.
- A **watershed** is the catchment area of a drainage basin.
- Streams pick up or dissolve some of the material they flow over, causing erosion. **Deposition** is when these materials fall to the stream bed.
- **Groundwater** is water present in saturated zones under Earth's surface, filling voids and cracks.
- **Karst** is surficial bedrock composed mainly of carbonate rock, such as limestone, that allows for the formation of large underground caverns and sinkholes.

- **Glaciers** are perennial ice masses formed by accumulation and compression of snow that survives year-round. Glaciers can grow large enough to flow downward, picking up material from one location and depositing it in another while altering the landscape in the process.
- **Seawater** contains large amounts of dissolved salts.
- **Waves** and **surface ocean currents** are generated by the frictional drag of winds across the surface of the water.
- **Tides** are caused by the gravitational pull from the sun and moon.
- The contact line between the ocean and land is called the **shoreline**.
- **Beaches** are portions of land where the ocean deposits sediment, called **coastal deposition**. **Coastal erosion** is typically found near a tectonic plate boundary, where ocean waves erode the coastline.
- **Corals** are marine animals (**polyps**) that grow in clear, shallow, sunlit ocean water. Corals have a hard exoskeleton formed from calcium carbonate. Corals depend on photosynthetic algae that generate food for the coral.
- **Salt marshes** and **mangrove swamps** are coastal areas where salt-tolerant plants grow and provide sheltered areas for fine-grained sediment and marine life. Corals, salt marshes, and mangrove swamps provide buffers between the ocean and coastline, protecting the coastline from erosion.
- **Deserts** are arid regions that receive very little precipitation. **Desert pavement** is coarse-grained particles such as gravel, hidden below the fine-grained particles of sand.
- Large deposits of sand can form windswept ridges called **dunes**. A desert covered by large swaths of dunes is called an **erg desert**.
- **Wind** is the horizontal movement of air across Earth's surface. Wind can cause erosion by **eolian particles** (materials eroded, transported, and deposited by winds) hitting solid rocks.
- The **water cycle** shows the various forms of water and the process of evaporation, precipitation, and collection. More than ninety-seven percent of Earth's water is found in the ocean. Most of Earth's fresh water is contained as ice in glaciers.
- **Planetary geology** is the application of geologic principles to celestial bodies such as moons or planets, using data collected by remote-sensing devices and human exploration.
- **Relative time** describes the order of events without assigning a specific date to them. **Relative dating** is the process of using relative time to describe the sequence of events that have shaped a particular area.
- **Absolute time** is used when a specific age can be assigned to an event such as a rock formation or volcanic eruption. This can be done using a method called **radiometric dating**, which analyzes the rate of decay of radioactive isotopes based on a characteristic half-life.

- The combination of relative and absolute time is called the **geologic time scale**.
- **Structural geology** is the study of processes that cause rock deformation and the effects caused by those processes. Many of these processes stem from the movement of tectonic plates.
- **Folding** is when compressive forces bend rock rather than breaking rock. This is a slow process involving high pressure and high temperature.
- A **fault** forms when rocks fracture and move past each other. The movement is usually a sudden release of energy resulting in an earthquake.
- A **volcano** is an opening in Earth's crust where lava erupts. Volcanoes typically form along tectonic plate boundaries where subduction is occurring or over hotspots where hot mantle material rises.
- **Hotspots** are areas where plumes of particularly hot mantle material rise, prompting volcanic activity at the surface.
- **Volcanic hazards** include ejections of rock, **lahars** (debris flows), **pyroclastic flows** (superheated gases and debris), landslides, lava flows, release of volcanic gases, and tsunamis.
- **Ores** are bodies of rock that contain useful elements or minerals in a concentration high enough to be mined economically. Salt, gypsum, gold, and iron are types of ores.
- Coal, oil, and natural gas are collectively known as **fossil fuels**. These are finite resources and using them releases pollutants into the air that can affect the climate.
- **Environmental geology** is the study of the interaction between the geologic environment and humankind. Of significant concern to environmental geologists is **global climate change**.
- **Climate** is the average atmospheric conditions for an area, such as rainfall and temperature. **Climatologists** use computer models based on past climate data to track changes and predict how human activity will affect climate in the future.
- **Paleoclimatology** is the study of past climates in order to better understand current and future climate changes and the effect they may cause.
- **Greenhouse gases** are radiatively active gases in Earth's atmosphere. These gases absorb and re-radiate longer wavelengths of solar radiation, which in turn keeps the planet warm and habitable. Adding greenhouse gases by burning fossil fuels causes an enhanced **greenhouse effect**, whereby the temperatures on Earth's surface increase. This can change rainfall patterns and affect the lifecycle of plants and animals, as well as cause colder winters and more severe weather patterns.

Chapter 4

Introduction to Geology Post-Test

POST-TEST ANSWER SHEET

1. Ⓐ Ⓑ Ⓒ Ⓓ	15. Ⓐ Ⓑ Ⓒ Ⓓ	29. Ⓐ Ⓑ Ⓒ Ⓓ
2. Ⓐ Ⓑ Ⓒ Ⓓ	16. Ⓐ Ⓑ Ⓒ Ⓓ	30. Ⓐ Ⓑ Ⓒ Ⓓ
3. Ⓐ Ⓑ Ⓒ Ⓓ	17. Ⓐ Ⓑ Ⓒ Ⓓ	31. Ⓐ Ⓑ Ⓒ Ⓓ
4. Ⓐ Ⓑ Ⓒ Ⓓ	18. Ⓐ Ⓑ Ⓒ Ⓓ	32. Ⓐ Ⓑ Ⓒ Ⓓ
5. Ⓐ Ⓑ Ⓒ Ⓓ	19. Ⓐ Ⓑ Ⓒ Ⓓ	33. Ⓐ Ⓑ Ⓒ Ⓓ
6. Ⓐ Ⓑ Ⓒ Ⓓ	20. Ⓐ Ⓑ Ⓒ Ⓓ	34. Ⓐ Ⓑ Ⓒ Ⓓ
7. Ⓐ Ⓑ Ⓒ Ⓓ	21. Ⓐ Ⓑ Ⓒ Ⓓ	35. Ⓐ Ⓑ Ⓒ Ⓓ
8. Ⓐ Ⓑ Ⓒ Ⓓ	22. Ⓐ Ⓑ Ⓒ Ⓓ	36. Ⓐ Ⓑ Ⓒ Ⓓ
9. Ⓐ Ⓑ Ⓒ Ⓓ	23. Ⓐ Ⓑ Ⓒ Ⓓ	37. Ⓐ Ⓑ Ⓒ Ⓓ
10. Ⓐ Ⓑ Ⓒ Ⓓ	24. Ⓐ Ⓑ Ⓒ Ⓓ	38. Ⓐ Ⓑ Ⓒ Ⓓ
11. Ⓐ Ⓑ Ⓒ Ⓓ	25. Ⓐ Ⓑ Ⓒ Ⓓ	39. Ⓐ Ⓑ Ⓒ Ⓓ
12. Ⓐ Ⓑ Ⓒ Ⓓ	26. Ⓐ Ⓑ Ⓒ Ⓓ	40. Ⓐ Ⓑ Ⓒ Ⓓ
13. Ⓐ Ⓑ Ⓒ Ⓓ	27. Ⓐ Ⓑ Ⓒ Ⓓ	41. Ⓐ Ⓑ Ⓒ Ⓓ
14. Ⓐ Ⓑ Ⓒ Ⓓ	28. Ⓐ Ⓑ Ⓒ Ⓓ	42. Ⓐ Ⓑ Ⓒ Ⓓ

43. Ⓐ Ⓑ Ⓒ Ⓓ   49. Ⓐ Ⓑ Ⓒ Ⓓ   55. Ⓐ Ⓑ Ⓒ Ⓓ

44. Ⓐ Ⓑ Ⓒ Ⓓ   50. Ⓐ Ⓑ Ⓒ Ⓓ   56. Ⓐ Ⓑ Ⓒ Ⓓ

45. Ⓐ Ⓑ Ⓒ Ⓓ   51. Ⓐ Ⓑ Ⓒ Ⓓ   57. Ⓐ Ⓑ Ⓒ Ⓓ

46. Ⓐ Ⓑ Ⓒ Ⓓ   52. Ⓐ Ⓑ Ⓒ Ⓓ   58. Ⓐ Ⓑ Ⓒ Ⓓ

47. Ⓐ Ⓑ Ⓒ Ⓓ   53. Ⓐ Ⓑ Ⓒ Ⓓ   59. Ⓐ Ⓑ Ⓒ Ⓓ

48. Ⓐ Ⓑ Ⓒ Ⓓ   54. Ⓐ Ⓑ Ⓒ Ⓓ   60. Ⓐ Ⓑ Ⓒ Ⓓ

INTRODUCTION TO GEOLOGY POST-TEST
72 minutes—60 questions

Directions: Carefully read each of the following 60 questions. Choose the best answer to each and fill in the corresponding circle on the answer sheet. The Answer Key and Explanations can be found following this post-test.

1. The planets of our outer solar system formed by the accretion of

   A. extrasolar planets.
   B. gas giant planets.
   C. rocky planetesimals.
   D. icy planetesimals.

2. Which of the following minerals is a member of the sulfide family?

   A. Sulfur
   B. Cinnabar
   C. Anhydrite
   D. Linarite

3. In what order do rocks move through the rock cycle?

   A. Igneous rocks break apart and then form sedimentary rocks, which become metamorphic rocks.
   B. Igneous rocks become metamorphic rocks, which break apart and then form sedimentary rocks.
   C. Metamorphic rocks melt and then cool into igneous rocks, which break apart and then form sedimentary rocks.
   D. Rocks do not follow any set path as they move through the rock cycle, which has no beginning or end.

4. What are the longest intervals in the geologic time scale?

   A. Eras
   B. Ages
   C. Eons
   D. Epochs

5. The lithosphere is made up of the crust and the

    A. asthenosphere.
    B. Mohorovičić discontinuity.
    C. uppermost part of the mantle.
    D. continents.

6. What seafloor feature marks a tectonic plate boundary at which subduction is taking place?

    A. Transform fault
    B. Seafloor spreading center
    C. Deep-ocean trench
    D. Mid-ocean ridge

7. In the formation of igneous rock, large mineral crystal size is most closely associated with the

    A. percentage of silica present.
    B. slow cooling of molten rock.
    C. high melting point of mafic minerals.
    D. viscosity of magma.

8. Which type of fold has the oldest rock at its center?

    A. Monocline
    B. Anticline
    C. Recumbent
    D. Syncline

9. Which layer of Earth is correctly matched with its average density?

    A. Oceanic crust—3.3 g/cm^3
    B. Outer core—13.0 g/cm^3
    C. Continental crust—2.7 g/cm^3
    D. Asthenosphere—5.6 g/cm^3

10. What is one way to determine whether a chain of oceanic islands may be the product of intraplate volcanism associated with a mantle plume?

    A. Calculate the volume of magma that would have to be generated by the mantle plume to form each island.
    B. Measure the distance between each island in the chain to determine how active the mantle plume has been over time.
    C. Determine whether the ages of the islands increase with distance from the most recently formed island.
    D. Analyze whether the spatial distribution of the islands is consistent with the locations of mantle convection currents.

11. What type of fault has a vertical fault plane?

    A. Strike-slip fault
    B. Reverse fault
    C. Normal fault
    D. Thrust fault

12. The dynamic balance between buoyancy and gravity that causes heavier portions of the lithosphere—such as regions with mountain ranges or continental glaciers—to sink deeper into the asthenosphere, and regions of lower density to float higher, is called

    A. elastic rebound.
    B. isostasy.
    C. orogeny.
    D. plastic deformation.

13. Volcanoes located far away from a tectonic plate boundary are associated with

    A. faulting.
    B. subduction.
    C. rifting.
    D. hotspots.

14. In a well-developed soil profile in a humid temperate region, the O, A, E, and B soil horizons comprise the solum. What is immediately below the solum?

    A. Regolith
    B. Plant roots
    C. Bedrock
    D. Subsoil

15. The evaporation of water can leave behind minerals that form what kind of rock?

    A. Clastic
    B. Igneous
    C. Metamorphic
    D. Sedimentary

16. What is a difference between a shield volcano and a composite volcano?

    A. A shield volcano produces lava that contains a higher percentage of silica.
    B. An eruption of a composite volcano tends to be effusive.
    C. A composite volcano is more likely to emit dangerous volcanic gases.
    D. The eruption of a shield volcano is not as dangerous to nearby human populations.

17. An event in which water-saturated sediments lose cohesion when shaken by an earthquake, causing the ground to flow, is called

    A. a lahar.
    B. a debris slide.
    C. liquefaction.
    D. slumping.

18. Which of the following rock types is matched with the correct classification?

    A. Coal (sedimentary)
    B. Shale (metamorphic)
    C. Gneiss (igneous)
    D. Quartzite (igneous)

19. A fast-moving, superheated mixture of gases and particles of rock ejected during a volcanic eruption that flows downslope is known as a

A. lahar.
B. tsunami.
C. pyroclastic flow.
D. landslide.

20. Metamorphic agents include

A. melting.
B. erosion and deposition.
C. recrystallization.
D. chemically active fluids.

21. Data recorded by a single seismograph can be used to calculate how far away an earthquake was because

A. surface waves travel faster than body waves.
B. P waves travel faster than S waves.
C. the data allow asperities to be precisely located.
D. the data allow for the triangulation of the earthquake's location.

22. What feature forms as a stream flowing into a larger body of water rapidly slows down, leading to the deposition of large amounts of sediment?

A. Point bar
B. Delta
C. Levee
D. Floodplain

23. A nonfoliated metamorphic rock is characterized by

A. the parallel alignment of platy minerals.
B. the ability to be readily split along cleavage planes.
C. randomly oriented mineral grains.
D. compositional banding.

24. The point on Earth's surface directly above the location inside Earth's crust where earthquake movement first occurs is called the

    A. epicenter.
    B. focus.
    C. Richter point.
    D. Mercalli point.

25. What processes in the rock cycle are most important in transforming igneous rock into clastic sedimentary rock?

    A. Intrusion and slow cooling
    B. Rifting and subduction
    C. Erosion, deposition, and lithification
    D. Evaporation, condensation, and precipitation

26. What is a common use of aggregate?

    A. To make pottery or to coat paper
    B. As a fossil fuel burned for heat
    C. As a source of economically valuable metals
    D. To mix with cement to produce concrete

27. A karst landscape may form in an area where the surficial bedrock is composed of

    A. basalt.
    B. granite.
    C. slate.
    D. limestone.

28. What is likely to happen to a metamorphic rock that becomes buried deep in the crust where it is subjected to high pressure and temperatures just below its melting point?

    A. It becomes an igneous rock and moves to another stage in the rock cycle.
    B. It changes into a different type of metamorphic rock.
    C. It lithifies into a new sedimentary rock.
    D. It undergoes uplift to Earth's surface, where it breaks down into sediments over time.

29. A valley that had an alpine glacier flowing down it at some histor-ical point in time has a characteristic

A. U-shape.
B. V-shape.
C. plane shape.
D. cone shape.

30. An environmental geologist is likely to be involved in the production of

A. earthquake predictions.
B. computer models used to study climate change.
C. environmental hazard maps.
D. improved radiometric dating techniques.

31. Where would you be likely to find igneous rock that is currently form-ing and recording the present direction of Earth's magnetic field?

A. Mid-Atlantic Ridge
B. Himalayan Mountains
C. Mount Everest
D. San Andreas fault system

32. Which of the following is a property of all greenhouse gases?

A. They absorb short-wavelength solar radiation.
B. They are radiatively active.
C. Their sources are entirely anthropogenic.
D. Their presence cools the atmosphere.

33. Longshore drift is the zig-zag movement of sediments along a(n)

A. atoll.
B. gyre.
C. moraine.
D. beach.

34. Which of the following fossil fuels is considered to burn the most cleanly because it produces the smallest amounts of pollutants?

A. Oil
B. Bituminous coal
C. Lignite
D. Natural gas

35. Silicate minerals, such as feldspars, combine with water, leading to the formation of clay minerals as part of which process?

A. Physical weathering
B. Mechanical weathering
C. Chemical weathering
D. Eluviation weathering

36. An example of a feature indicating that erosion is the dominant process occurring along a coastline is a

A. sea arch.
B. tombolo.
C. barrier island.
D. spit.

37. The study of interactions between humans and the geologic environment is the focus of

A. climatology.
B. stratigraphy.
C. environmental geology.
D. structural geology.

38. How are minerals classified into families?

A. By composition
B. By crystalline structure
C. By physical properties such as hardness
D. According to how they form

39. Eolian materials have been eroded, transported, and deposited by

A. the movement of water.
B. glacial ice.
C. winds.
D. fluvial processes.

40. A talus cone is likely to form as a result of

A. volcanic eruptions.
B. rockfalls.
C. debris flows.
D. fluvial processes.

41. Which of the following contains more than 97 percent of Earth's water?

    A. Aquifers
    B. Streams and lakes
    C. Oceans
    D. Glaciers

42. According to Bowen's reaction series, which of the following minerals would form earliest as a mafic magma cooled?

    A. Amphibole
    B. Biotite mica
    C. Olivine
    D. Orthoclase feldspar

43. The smallest solid material that can be carried by a stream is transported as part of its

    A. bedload.
    B. traction load.
    C. solution load.
    D. suspended load.

44. When geologists describe the sequence of geologic events that have shaped an area, without assigning dates in years before present to the events, they are using the technique of

    A. radiometric dating.
    B. relative dating.
    C. isotopic dating.
    D. absolute dating.

45. Cockpit karst is characterized by the presence of numerous

    A. karst valleys.
    B. stalactites and stalagmites.
    C. sinkholes.
    D. oxbows and meanders.

46. What does "the present is the key to the past," meaning that the geologic processes acting today are the same ones that have been acting throughout geologic time, refer to?

    A. Punctuated equilibrium
    B. Fossil succession
    C. Superposition
    D. Uniformitarianism

47. An extensive layer of glacial sediment deposited in front of a glacier by meltwater streams forms a(n)

    A. outwash plain.
    B. erratic.
    C. roche moutonnée.
    D. drumlin.

48. What type of forces cause folded mountains to form along an oceanic–continental convergent boundary?

    A. Compressive
    B. Tensional
    C. Shearing
    D. Frictional

49. How do granite and rhyolite differ?

    A. Granite has a more felsic composition, whereas rhyolite has a more mafic composition.
    B. Granite has a coarse-grained texture, whereas rhyolite has a fine-grained texture.
    C. Granite is an intrusive igneous rock, whereas rhyolite is a metamorphic rock.
    D. Granite is an extrusive igneous rock, whereas rhyolite is an intrusive igneous rock.

50. What depositional feature marks the farthest extent reached by a glacier?

    A. End moraine
    B. Medial moraine
    C. Ground moraine
    D. Terminal moraine

51. Which of the following is important in the formation of the submarine mountain ranges that make up Earth's mid-ocean ridge system?

   A. Collision of tectonic plates
   B. Thermal inflation of oceanic crust
   C. Folding and thickening of continental crust
   D. Movement of blocks of rock along reverse and thrust faults

52. Which of the following rock types contains sediments likely to be deposited in a high-energy environment?

   A. Schist
   B. Shale
   C. Sandstone
   D. Conglomerate

53. Before it erupts, molten rock rises and collects under a volcano in a

   A. crater.
   B. caldera.
   C. pluton.
   D. magma chamber.

54. Eccentricity, the 100,000-year component of the Milankovitch cycles, involves

   A. changes in Earth's orbit from more circular to more elliptical and back again.
   B. the amount of tilt of Earth's axis, which varies between about 22.1° and 24.5°.
   C. the "wobble" of Earth's axis, which can be compared to the wobble of a spinning toy top.
   D. slow changes in the locations of continents and the configuration of ocean basins over time.

55. Which factor is most important in causing ocean tides?

   A. The moon's gravitational influence
   B. The sun's gravitational influence
   C. The configuration of the seafloor
   D. The configuration of the shoreline

56. Which type of evidence present in a sedimentary rock gives information about the types of plants that were growing in the region when the sediments were deposited?

A. Preserved mud cracks
B. Pollen grains
C. Preserved ripple marks
D. Grain size of the sediments

57. What type of volcano is formed by repeated effusive eruptions of low-viscosity, basaltic lava?

A. Shield volcano
B. Composite volcano
C. Lava dome volcano
D. Cinder cone volcano

58. The ground surface of subtropical deserts is frequently characterized by the presence of

A. sand dunes.
B. erg formations.
C. desert pavement.
D. slipface surfaces.

59. When a shale undergoes metamorphosis, what new types of rock will form, in order from low-grade to high-grade metamorphism?

A. Shale → slate → phyllite → schist → gneiss
B. Shale → phyllite → slate → gneiss → schist
C. Shale → slate → schist → gneiss → phyllite
D. Shale → slate → schist → phyllite → gneiss

60. In the water cycle, what is meant by precipitation?

A. All forms of atmospheric moisture, including water vapor
B. Rain, sleet, snow, and hail
C. Water that is carried by advection from the ocean to land
D. Evaporation, sublimation, and transpiration

ANSWER KEY AND EXPLANATIONS

1. D	13. D	25. C	37. C	49. B
2. B	14. A	26. D	38. A	50. D
3. D	15. D	27. D	39. C	51. B
4. C	16. D	28. B	40. B	52. D
5. C	17. C	29. A	41. C	53. D
6. C	18. A	30. C	42. C	54. A
7. B	19. C	31. A	43. D	55. A
8. B	20. D	32. B	44. B	56. B
9. C	21. B	33. D	45. C	57. A
10. C	22. B	34. D	46. D	58. C
11. A	23. C	35. C	47. A	59. A
12. B	24. A	36. A	48. A	60. B

1. **The correct answer is D.** In the early solar system, cooler temperatures in the outer part of the disk of material surrounding the sun led to the formation of icy planetesimals, and the accretion of icy planetesimals resulted in the formation of the gas giant planets—Jupiter, Saturn, Neptune, and Uranus. Extrasolar planets (choice A) are planets that are not in our solar system. While the planets of the outer solar system are gas giant planets, choice B is incorrect because individual gas giants did not accrete to form larger ones. Choice C is incorrect because the accretion of rocky planetesimals led to the formation of the planets in the inner solar system—Mercury, Venus, Earth, and Mars.

2. **The correct answer is B.** In minerals of the sulfide family, sulfur combines with elements other than oxygen. Pyrite is an example of a sulfide mineral. Sulfur (choice A) is a native element mineral. Anhydrite and linarite (choices C and D) are sulfate minerals.

3. **The correct answer is D.** Processes in the rock cycle can occur in any order, including multiple cycles of igneous, metamorphic, or sedimentary processes involving the same body of rock before the rock moves to any other stage of the rock cycle. Choices A, B, and C are incorrect because they state a definite order of events.

4. The correct answer is C. The first and longest subdivisions of the geologic time scale are called eons. Choice A is incorrect because eons are divided into eras that are further divided into periods. Choice B is incorrect because epochs are divided into ages. Choice D is incorrect because periods are divided into epochs.

5. The correct answer is C. The crust and the cool rock of the uppermost part of the mantle form the lithosphere, which is broken into huge, slowly moving tectonic plates. The asthenosphere (choice A) is the portion of the upper mantle immediately below the lithosphere. The Mohorovičić discontinuity (choice B), also known as Moho, marks the boundary between the crust and uppermost mantle. Continents (choice D) are part of the crust.

6. The correct answer is C. Subduction occurs along a convergent tectonic plate boundary in a subduction zone, which is marked at the seafloor surface by a deep-ocean trench. A transform fault (choice A) is characteristic of a transform tectonic plate boundary, where no subduction occurs. A seafloor spreading center (choice B) and a mid-ocean ridge (choice D) are characteristic of a divergent tectonic plate boundary in the ocean.

7. The correct answer is B. The size of the mineral crystals in an igneous rock is controlled by the rock's cooling history—slower cooling leads to larger crystals. The percentage of silica (choice A) is important in determining the types of minerals that form (mafic, intermediate, or felsic) but not their size. Choice C is incorrect because the melting point of a mineral determines the temperature at which it crystalizes, but not its size. The viscosity of magma (choice D) determines how readily it flows and whether a volcanic eruption is effusive or explosive.

8. The correct answer is B. In an anticline, rock layers form an arch where the oldest rock is at the center. A monocline (choice A) is characterized by a single bend in rock layers and therefore does not really have a center. A recumbent fold (choice C) is an anticline or syncline that has been turned on its side. In a syncline (choice D), layers of rock resemble a nested set of bowls, and the youngest rock is at the center.

9. The correct answer is C. Continental crust has the lowest density of any of Earth's layers. Choice A is incorrect because the average density of oceanic crust is 3.0 g/cm^3. Choice B is incorrect because the density of the outer core ranges between 9.9 and 12.2 g/cm^3. Choice D is incorrect because the average density of the asthenosphere is 3.3 g/cm^3.

10. The correct answer is C. The youngest island produced by intraplate volcanism is the one currently above the mantle plume, and the other islands are increasingly older the farther they are away from that point. Choice A is incorrect because the volume of magma produced determines how large a volcano grows and whether it becomes tall enough for its top to become an island. Choice B is incorrect because the distance between islands can allow the rate of plate movement to be calculated but does not indicate whether the islands are products of intraplate volcanism. If the islands form a line, that can suggest formation due to intraplate volcanism, but choice D is incorrect because this information does not provide evidence about the locations of mantle convection currents, whose rising and sinking limbs are associated with tectonic plate boundaries.

11. The correct answer is A. A strike-slip fault, also called a transform fault, has a vertical fault plane along which the blocks of rock on either side move horizontally past one another. A reverse fault (choice B), normal fault (choice C), and thrust fault (choice D) all have an inclined fault plane along which motion with a vertical component occurs.

12. The correct answer is B. The equilibrium between buoyancy and gravity that causes lithospheric plates to "float" on the underlying, denser asthenosphere is called isostasy. Because geologic processes are slowly but constantly causing large-scale changes to Earth's surface, slow isostatic adjustments are constantly taking place. The elastic-rebound theory (choice A) describes how deformed rock on either side of a fault snaps back, or rebounds, into its original configuration when accumulated energy is released in an earthquake. An orogeny (choice C) is a mountain-building event. Ductile, or plastic deformation, in the asthenosphere (choice D) allows for convection and the movement of the overlying lithospheric plates.

13. **The correct answer is D.** A hotspot is an area where a plume of particularly hot mantle material rises, promoting volcanism at Earth's surface. Choice A is incorrect because faulting and volcanic activity can occur in the same area, but both are usually associated with dynamics at plate tectonic boundaries. Subduction (choice B) and rifting (choice C) are processes that occur at tectonic plate boundaries.

14. **The correct answer is A.** The solum, or true soil, is underlain by partially weathered and broken bedrock called regolith. Plant roots (choice B) and animal life are found in the solum. Unbroken bedrock (choice C) underlies regolith. Choice D is incorrect because the B horizon of the solum is also referred to as the subsoil.

15. **The correct answer is D.** Chemical sedimentary rocks form as minerals precipitate from water, such as when a shallow ocean basin or a mineral-rich lake dries up. Clastic sedimentary rocks (choice A) are made of particles originating from earlier rocks. Igneous rocks (choice B) form as molten rock cools. Metamorphic rocks (choice C) form as heat or pressure transforms an existing rock into another type of rock.

16. **The correct answer is D.** The effusive eruptions commonly produced by shield volcanoes may result in extensive lava flows, but unlike the explosive eruptions of composite volcanoes, they rarely cause injury or death to humans. Choice A is incorrect because the lava of a shield volcano has a basaltic composition and, therefore, is relatively depleted in silica. Choice B is incorrect because a composite volcano tends to produce explosive eruptions. Choice C is incorrect because both shield volcanoes and composite volcanoes emit dangerous gases.

17. **The correct answer is C.** Liquefaction is a type of earthflow in which water-saturated sediments lose cohesion and act like a liquid, causing any buildings present to tilt or sink into the ground. A lahar (choice A) is a volcanic mudflow that occurs when sediments and volcanic debris mix with water and move downslope. A debris slide (choice B) occurs when a mass of rock, or a mass of mainly soil and regolith, slides downslope while remaining in a fairly coherent block. Slumping (choice D) occurs when surface material remains in a fairly coherent block as it moves downslope along a curved surface.

18. **The correct answer is A.** Coal is a sedimentary rock formed from the carbon-rich remains of ancient plants that have been transformed by heat and pressure. Shale (choice B) is a clastic sedimentary rock. Gneiss and quartzite (choices C and D) are metamorphic rocks.

19. **The correct answer is C.** A pyroclastic flow is a cloud of extremely hot gases and pyroclastic particles dense enough to hug the ground and race down the slopes of a volcano at tremendous speeds, burning or burying everything in its path. A lahar (choice A) is a type of volcanic debris flow, but it does not sustain the high temperatures of a pyroclastic flow. Choice B is incorrect because tsunami waves are created by the eruption of an underwater volcano, an eruption-triggered landslide that cascades into the ocean, or an underwater earthquake. A landslide (choice D) is a type of mass wasting event that may occur on a volcano but is not necessarily associated with volcanoes.

20. **The correct answer is D.** Chemically active fluids can cause minerals to dissolve and then precipitate in a different location or cause ion exchanges that alter the overall composition of the rock they are circulating through. Choice A is incorrect because if melting occurs, the result is an igneous rock, not a metamorphic one. Erosion and deposition (choice B) are processes important in the formation of sedimentary rocks. Recrystallization (choice C) is a frequent result of metamorphic processes, not a cause of them.

21. **The correct answer is B.** The difference in initial arrival times of the faster-moving P waves and slower-moving S waves as recorded by a seismograph is used to calculate how far away an earthquake was. The opposite of choice A is true. Surface waves travel more slowly than either type of body wave. Choice C is incorrect because an asperity is a localized area of high strain along a fault that can rupture to produce an earthquake, but the actual point where movement first occurs is called the earthquake focus or hypocenter. Choice D is incorrect because data from at least three seismic stations are needed to triangulate an earthquake's location.

22. **The correct answer is B.** As water leaves a stream channel and enters a larger body of water, it spreads out and slows down, causing sediment to be deposited that builds up into a delta. A point bar (choice A) is a depositional feature that builds up in a meandering stream where water flow slows along the inner part of a meander. Levees (choice C) are depositional features that form and grow as a stream overflows during a flood, causing coarse sediments to be deposited adjacent to the channel, which builds up the stream's banks. A floodplain (choice D) is a depositional feature that forms as successive flood events deposit layers of fine-grained sediments, leading to the formation of a relatively smooth, low-lying plain on either side of a stream channel.

23. **The correct answer is C.** Lack of foliation, characterized by randomly oriented mineral grains, indicates that a metamorphic rock has undergone at most only minor deformation and may also have a limited chemical composition. Choices A, B, and D are all possible characteristics of foliated metamorphic rocks that have been subjected to differential stress.

24. **The correct answer is A.** The point on a fault plane where movement first occurs during an earthquake is called the focus or hypocenter; the point on Earth's surface directly above the focus is called the epicenter. The focus (choice B) is located within the crust. The Richter scale (choice C) is a logarithmic scale that provides a single numeric measure of earthquake intensity. The Mercalli scale (choice D) is used to describe earthquake damage at particular locations.

25. **The correct answer is C.** Erosion transports particles (sediments) broken off of rock; deposition can lead to extensive accumulations of sediments; and lithification is the process by which sedimentary deposits form sedimentary rock. Intrusion and slow cooling (choice A) are important in the formation of igneous rock. Rifting and subduction (choice B) are tectonic processes, not processes in the rock cycle. Evaporation, condensation, and precipitation (choice D) are processes that are important in the hydrologic cycle or, in the case of evaporation and chemical precipitation, in the formation of chemical sedimentary rock.

26. **The correct answer is D.** Deposits of aggregate (sand and gravel) are a common source of the hard material that is mixed with a cementing material to produce mortar, plaster, or concrete. Choice A is incorrect because it is clay minerals that are important for the making of pottery or as a coating for paper. Choice B is incorrect because aggregate is not combustible. Choice C is incorrect because mineral resources containing economically valuable metals are called ores.

27. **The correct answer is D.** Bedrock that is primarily composed of a carbonate rock such as limestone is prone to chemical weathering by carbonation, leading to the development of a karst landscape. Basalt (choice A), granite (choice B), and slate (choice C) are not carbonate rocks.

28. **The correct answer is B.** A metamorphic rock can be transformed by heat and pressure into a different type of metamorphic rock while remaining in the solid state. Choice A is incorrect because melting must occur before a new igneous rock forms. Choice C is incorrect because heat and pressure are metamorphic agents, not sedimentary ones. Choice D is incorrect because conditions of high pressures and temperatures cause metamorphism, not uplift.

29. The correct answer is A. The enormous erosive power of a glacier creates a broad valley with steep sides, characteristic of a U-shape. Choice B is characteristic of a stream-cut valley. Choice C is incorrect because a valley is an elongated area of relatively low-lying land with higher elevations on either side; these variations in elevation mean that a valley cannot be a flat plane. Choice D is incorrect because a valley is elongated, not circular like the base of a cone, and the sides of a valley do not slope inward over the valley floor.

30. The correct answer is C. Environmental geologists collect, synthesize, and present information in ways that are useful for policy makers and the general public; one of the ways they present information is by producing environmental hazard maps. Choice A is incorrect because although environmental geologists may use earthquake predictions to produce seismic hazard maps, they are unlikely to generate the predictions themselves. Choice B is incorrect because climatologists are the scientists who produce and use computer models to study climate. Choice D is incorrect because developing radiometric dating techniques, which involves measuring the relative amounts of a radioactive isotope and its daughter isotope present in a rock, is an unlikely pursuit for an environmental geologist.

31. The correct answer is A. Newly formed oceanic crust, which contains mafic magnetic minerals that record the direction of Earth's magnetic field, is constantly forming as fresh magma rises, cools, and is moved away from the Mid-Atlantic Ridge by seafloor spreading. The Himalayas (choice B) are a product of the collision boundary between India and Asia, a process that is not associated with current igneous activity. Mount Everest (choice C) is part of the Himalayas. The San Andreas fault system (choice D) is a transform boundary that separates the Pacific Plate from the North American Plate. Volcanism is not associated with transform boundaries.

32. **The correct answer is B.** Greenhouse gases are radiatively active gases, which means they absorb and reradiate energy at the longer wavelengths of the infrared radiation released from Earth's surface. Choice A is incorrect because greenhouse gases are transparent to short-wavelength radiation from the sun that reaches Earth's surface. Choice C is incorrect because greenhouse gases have natural as well as anthropogenic (human-caused) sources. Choice D is incorrect because greenhouse gases warm Earth's surface and the air in contact with it by delaying the escape of infrared energy to space.

33. **The correct answer is D.** A longshore current transports large quantities of sand and other sediments along a beach as longshore drift; the particles of sediment move in a zig-zag fashion as they are pushed landward by advancing waves and pulled seaward by retreating waves. An atoll (choice A) is a ring of coral surrounding a central lagoon. Surface currents in the open ocean form large, roughly circular patterns of flow called gyres (choice B). A moraine (choice C) is a deposit of glacial till that forms along the sides or at the end of a glacier.

34. **The correct answer is D.** When natural gas burns, it produces almost no sulfur dioxide emissions and much smaller emissions of pollutants such as nitrogen oxide and particulates compared to emission from oil or coal. Choices A, B, and C are incorrect because oil or coal, including bituminous coal and lignite, produce more pollutants when burned.

35. **The correct answer is C.** Feldspar minerals combine with water to form clay minerals by hydrolysis, which is a chemical weathering process. Physical weathering (choice A) and mechanical weathering (choice B) are terms referring to the same set of processes by which rock is broken apart with no change in mineral composition. Eluviation (choice D) is the process by which fine materials such as clays are removed to lower soil horizons.

36. **The correct answer is A.** Sea arches form when openings are eroded into detached or semi-detached bodies of rock near a coastline. Tombolos (choice B), barrier islands (choice C), and spits (choice D) are depositional features.

37. **The correct answer is C.** Environmental geology is concerned with interactions between humans and the geologic environment and calls on knowledge and techniques from all branches of geology to identify and, to the extent possible, remediate environmental problems. Climatology (choice A) is the study of climate. Stratigraphy (choice B) involves the study of rock layers and their placement on relative and absolute time scales. Structural geology (choice D) is the study of processes that cause rock deformation as well as the effects of these processes.

38. **The correct answer is A.** Minerals are classified according to their composition into groups called families, the largest of which is the silicate family. Choice B is incorrect because while each mineral has a regular, repeating crystalline structure, this structure is not used to classify minerals by family. Physical properties (choice C) are used to identify individual minerals but are not used to identify the family each belongs to. Choice D is incorrect because rocks, not minerals, are classified according to how they form.

39. **The correct answer is C.** Eolian (also spelled aeolian) materials are those that have been eroded, transported, and deposited by winds. Water (choice A) is not a factor. Glacially transported sediments (choice B) are known as till. Fluvial processes (choice D) relate to stream systems.

40. **The correct answer is B.** Rockfalls occur when individual, detached pieces of rock travel at a high rate of speed down a very steep slope; they often result in an accumulation of a large pile of broken rocks called a talus cone. Choice A is incorrect because a rockfall is a mass wasting event, not a volcanic one. A debris flow (choice C) is a mixture of water, soil, and regolith that flows like a viscous fluid; when a debris flow stops moving, it does not form a rock pile. Fluvial processes (choice D) are associated with streamflow, not mass wasting events.

41. **The correct answer is C.** Almost all of Earth's water is contained in the oceans, which cover the majority of the planet's surface. Aquifers (choice A) are sediment layers and bodies of rock through which groundwater can flow, and groundwater is not even the largest component of Earth's freshwater. Choice B is incorrect because only a small percentage of Earth's water is present at any one time in streams and lakes. Although most of Earth's freshwater is contained as ice in glaciers, choice D is incorrect because most of the water on the planet is saline seawater.

42. **The correct answer is C.** Olivine forms early in the crystallization of a mafic magma because it crystallizes at high temperatures. Amphibole (choice A), biotite mica (choice B), and orthoclase feldspar (choice D) crystallize at lower temperatures.

43. **The correct answer is D.** The suspended load is made up of particles small enough to move with the flow of the water above the stream bed. Particles too coarse to be part of the suspended load may move along the stream bed as bedload (choice A); traction (choice B) is one way that bedload sediments move. The total load of dissolved sediments in a stream makes up its solution load (choice C).

44. **The correct answer is B.** A relative time scale describes the order in which events happened but does not assign dates to the events. The use of a relative time scale is called relative dating. Radiometric dating (choice A), also called isotopic dating (choice C), uses the half-lives of radioactive isotopes to determine numerical ages. Absolute dating (choice D) involves assigning a date in years before the present to an event.

45. **The correct answer is C.** Large numbers of sinkholes may be present in areas with well-developed karst topography; when the surface is heavily pitted by sinkholes, the resulting landscape is referred to as cockpit karst. Karst valleys (choice A) are larger features than sinkholes. Stalactites and stalagmites (choice B) are structures that form in underground caverns. Oxbows and meanders (choice D) are features associated with meandering streams.

46. **The correct answer is D.** The principle of uniformitarianism states that geologic processes that are active today can be applied to the interpretation of the geological record. The concept of punctuated equilibrium (choice A) describes how the usual flow of events within uniformitarianism can be briefly interrupted by quick changes. Determining fossil succession (choice B) is a technique by which scientists compare the relative ages of fossils found in different layers of rock in the same area as part of relative dating. The principle of superposition (choice C) states that layers of undisturbed rocks and sediments are always arranged with the youngest beds near and at the top of a sequence and the oldest at the base.

47. **The correct answer is A.** Deposits of glacial sediments that have been transported and sorted according to size by meltwater streams are called outwash, and a large area covered with outwash in front of a glacier forms an outwash plain. An erratic (choice B) is a boulder left behind by a glacier. A roche moutonnée (choice C) is an asymmetric hill that forms from the glacial erosion of bedrock. A drumlin (choice D) is an elongated hill formed by the deposition and molding of glacial sediments.

48. **The correct answer is A.** Along an oceanic–continental convergent boundary, compressive forces cause folded mountains to form as the plates move toward one another. Tensional forces (choice B) characterize divergent tectonic boundaries, where plates move away from one another. Shearing forces (choice C) characterize transform tectonic boundaries, where plates move horizontally past one another. Frictional forces (choice D) are important in preventing the blocks of rock on either side of a fault from moving until overcome by accumulated strain.

49. **The correct answer is B.** Granite, an intrusive igneous rock, cools more slowly than rhyolite, an extrusive igneous rock, and therefore has time for larger mineral crystals to form. Choice A is incorrect because granite and rhyolite are both felsic in composition. Choice C is incorrect because granite and rhyolite are both igneous rocks. The opposite of choice D is true. Granite is an intrusive igneous rock, and rhyolite is an extrusive igneous rock.

50. **The correct answer is D.** An end moraine that forms at the farthest extent reached by a glacier is called a terminal moraine. An end moraine (choice A) forms when till is deposited at the front of a glacier that has reached an equilibrium position, where glacial advance and retreat are balanced. A medial moraine (choice B) forms when two separate glaciers meet and flow in parallel, trapping their lateral moraines between them. A ground moraine (choice C) is a widespread deposit that forms as till drops to the ground from ice melting in place.

51. **The correct answer is B.** Heat from magma rising at a mid-ocean ridge causes thermal inflation of oceanic crust, helping to elevate the ridge above the surrounding seafloor. Choice A is incorrect because a mid-ocean ridge marks a region of tectonic divergence, not convergence. Choice C is incorrect because a mid-ocean ridge has oceanic crust; in addition, continental crust undergoes folding and thickening at a continental–continental collision boundary. Choice D is incorrect because active reverse and thrust faults are common at convergent tectonic boundaries, not divergent ones.

52. **The correct answer is D.** Accumulations of pebble-sized or larger sediments occur in high-energy environments, such as a fast-flowing mountain stream, from which only coarse-grained sediments can settle; lithification of such deposits produces conglomerate. Schist (choice A) is a metamorphic rock. Shale (choice B) is a fine-grained sedimentary rock that reflects a low-energy environment at the time of deposition. Sandstone (choice C) is a sedimentary rock that reflects a moderate-energy depositional environment.

53. **The correct answer is D.** Under a volcano, magma rises and collects in an area called a magma chamber. When conditions are right, magma rises through conduits in the volcano and erupts as lava at the surface. A crater (choice A) is a roughly circular depression at the summit of a volcano. A caldera (choice B) is created at the surface when a large eruption partially empties the magma chamber and the suddenly unsupported top of the volcano collapses downward, forming a large, roughly circular basin. A pluton (choice C) is a large body of igneous rock that has cooled within the crust.

54. **The correct answer is A.** The Milankovitch cycles are a set of three interacting astronomical factors that affect the distribution of insolation at Earth's surface, and therefore climate. Eccentricity is the 100,000-year cycle of changes in the shape of Earth's orbit. Axial tilt describes the amount of tilt of Earth's axis, which varies on about a 40,000-year cycle (choice B). Precession describes the "wobble" of Earth's axis, which has a cycle of about 26,000 years (choice C). Although the locations of continents and the configuration of ocean basins are important factors influencing the development and ending of an ice age, they are controlled by plate tectonic processes, not Milankovitch cycles (choice D).

55. **The correct answer is A.** The gravitational pull experienced by Earth from both the sun and moon generates tides, but the moon's influence is more important because the moon is much closer. Choice B is incorrect because even though the sun is much larger than the moon, it is much farther away, so its gravitational influence is less. Choices C and D are incorrect because the configuration of the seafloor and shoreline influences the tidal range but does not generate tides.

56. The correct answer is B. Microscopic pollen grains incorporated into sedimentary strata yield information about the types of plants that were growing in the region, which provides information about the climate at the time of deposition. Preserved mud cracks (choice A) indicate that surficial sediments became desiccated and shrank in volume but do not indicate anything about plant types that may have been present. Preserved ripple marks (choice C) in sandstone indicate that before lithification occurred, sand was migrating along a surface, such as a beach or stream channel. Choice D is incorrect because sediment grain size indicates the energy of the depositional environment.

57. The correct answer is A. The low, mounded shape of a shield volcano forms as effusive eruptions produce large amounts of low-viscosity, basaltic lava, adding new layers of lava to the volcanic edifice. A composite volcano (choice B), also called a stratovolcano, is built up of accumulations of solid volcanic debris ejected during eruptions, interlayered with hardened flows of viscous lava. A lava dome (choice C) forms from high-viscosity lava with little ability to flow. A cinder cone (choice D) is a small volcano that forms as gas-rich lava is fragmented during an eruption, and pieces of lava thrown into the air cool and solidify as they descend. These pieces, called cinders, accumulate around the vent, causing a small, conical hill to form.

58. The correct answer is C. Desert pavement, which is a surface of coarse sediments resembling a cobblestone street, is common in deserts, especially in subtropical areas. Sand dunes (choice A) have no particular association with subtropical deserts. Choice B is incorrect because an erg desert is an extensive area of desert covered by sand dunes. A slipface (choice D) is the side of a dune along which sand grains tumble down after being pushed up the other side by winds.

59. **The correct answer is A.** Low-grade metamorphism transforms shale, a fine-grained sedimentary rock, into slate, a low-grade metamorphic rock; as metamorphism continues, slate transforms into phyllite, then schist, and finally, gneiss. Choice B is incorrect because slate is lower in metamorphic grade than phyllite. Choice C is incorrect because schist and gneiss are higher in metamorphic grade than phyllite. Choice D is incorrect because schist is higher in metamorphic grade than phyllite.

60. **The correct answer is B.** Precipitation transfers water from the atmosphere to Earth's surface in the form of rain or ice particles such as sleet, snow, or hail. Choice A is incorrect because it is the transfer of water from the atmosphere to Earth's surface, not just the presence of water that comprises precipitation; in addition, water vapor must condense before it becomes a form of precipitation. Choice C is incorrect because, although water advected from the ocean to land can fall as precipitation, precipitation is not the lateral transfer of water. Choice D is incorrect because evaporation, sublimation, and transpiration involve changes among the liquid, solid, and gaseous states of water but are not forms of precipitation.

Printed in the USA
CPSIA information can be obtained
at www.ICGtesting.com
JSHW012042140824
68134JS00033B/3209

9 780768 944679